D1597221

HISTORY OF
FASHION

New Look to Now

HISTORY OF
FASHION

New Look to Now

JUNE MARSH

VIVAYS PUBLISHING

This book is dedicated to my husband,
Graham Marsh

Published by Vivays Publishing Ltd
www.vivays-publishing.com

A catalogue record for this book is available from the British Library.

ISBN   978-1-908126-21-4

Publishing Director: Lee Ripley
Designer: Ian Hunt
Front cover: © Dominique Charrioau/WireImage
Back cover: © Erwin Blumenfeld/Condé Nast Archive/Corbis
Printed in China

Contents

Preface

When I became a fashion editor in the 1970s, Paris couture was sidelined by ready-to-wear, which dominated the catwalks of Milan, Paris, New York and London. It was exciting and inspirational and lived up to all my expectations. All the magic of the fashion show, the music, the lights, the models was thrilling, plus the possibility of meeting the designers at a club or party afterwards added to the sense of occasion and the feeling of being at one with your world. Ideas flowed and I could not wait to get back to London to tell everyone about it and attempt to recreate some of the magic on my own fashion pages. Trips to these international shows were what fuelled fashion insiders. In those pre-Internet days the world went at a slower place, which meant there was time to discuss and consider the collections we'd just seen before filing our report in a very civilised manner – usually over a glass of wine at dinner.

In New York we found the slick, minimalist designs of Calvin Klein refreshing, Ralph Lauren's sophisticated take on country clothes comforting and Perry Ellis's reworking of preppy style reassuringly youthful. In Milan, Giorgio Armani was king, and the insouciance of the soft tailoring and muted colours of Cerrutti, Basile, Missoni and Max Mara were quintessentially Italian. But without a doubt, it was in Paris where the most 'happening' catwalk shows were performed.

In Paris Yves Saint Laurent's star was shining brightest. With each collection he produced a more brilliant and unforgettable experience than before. Kenzo Takada presented joyous and youthful styles that opened a whole new world of costume and dreams. Sonia Rykiel and Dorothée Bis had become the first word in knitwear. Pablo and Delia were a Brazilian couple that epitomised the mood of the time with their painterly designs and we saw the romantic side of Karl Lagerfeld at Chloé. Back in London we had our own national treasures, among them Zandra Rhodes, Jean Muir, Biba, Margaret Howell and Ossie Clarke.

Throughout the prosperous eighties and nineties couture once more reigned supreme with exciting new couturiers such as Christian Lacroix, Jean Paul Gaultier, Vivienne Westwood, Gianni Versace, John Galliano and Alexander McQueen to refresh and reinvigorate fashion's ever-changing scene.

And today, fashion has reached a new status accepted both academically and as an art form. It is a massive global industry where brand choice is paramount, whether it is at couture or high street level. Indeed, the same designer names appear on both.

The Internet has opened a whole new digital world where even if you live in the remotest part of the globe you can buy the latest offering from fashion's finest. Reporting the trends has become a free-for-all where bloggers and twitterers have, arguably, as much advertising power as the professional.

The world of fashion, with its many diverse and interesting characters, is never dull and remains one of the essential industries that rely on creative talent and innovative ideas to evolve and prosper. Brilliant new designers continue to restore the faith, just as Dior and Balenciaga did so convincingly in the 1950s.

June Marsh

Dior and the New Look

"God help the buyers who bought before they saw Dior! This changes everything."

CARMEL SNOW, *Harper's Bazaar*

The light was thin and the air freezing in Paris on the morning of February 12, 1947. It was Europe's coldest winter since 1870 and the city was still suffering from wartime shortages. There was little fuel, electricity was rationed and the streets were covered in snow.

The Paris couture trade, which had dominated international fashion since the late 18th century, was in a precarious state. French newspapers were on strike and the majority of American buyers were on their way home, not wishing to stay in Paris outside of the official schedule and having already completed business with the established couture houses.

A small crowd had gathered outside the courtyard doors of 30 Avenue Montaigne; elegantly dressed women in square-shouldered, knee-length fur coats and elaborate hats waited impatiently for the debut haute couture collection of the much talked-about, but little-known, Christian Dior.

Everything was completely new at the house of Dior; the hammering had only just finished as the first guests arrived. Fashionable decorator Victor Grandpierre had designed the interior in classic white and pearl grey. Tall windows were dressed flamboyantly with grey satin drapes and festooned blinds.

OPPOSITE This is the iconic New Look ensemble, a tailored suit with nipped-in waist and full skirt called – the Bar suit.

RIGHT 30 Avenue Montaigne in Paris, the building where the House of Dior is still based.

LEFT Front row at a 1955 Dior collection in Paris. Centre front: Marie-Louise Bousquet, Carmel Snow and Alexander Liberman.

RIGHT A blue silk taffeta Dior dinner dress with inverted flowers design, from the New Look collection of spring/summer 1947.

Crystal chandeliers hung from the high ceiling, Louis XIV style chairs were painted white and tall ashtrays were positioned conveniently around the room. In the centre of the room was just enough floor space for the models to perform a twirl or suitable pose.

Among the few remaining in Paris that morning were the esteemed editor-in-chief of US *Harper's Bazaar*, Carmel Snow; Marie-Louise Bousquet of their French desk and new *Bazaar* recruit, Ernestine Carter, a young fashion editor who was in Paris on her first assignment at the couture. A British journalist, Janet Ironside was also there, and Dior's old friend Michel de Brunhoff, manager of French *Vogue*. Paul Caldagues and Lucien and Cosette Vogel of the *Jardin des Modes* as well as Alice Chavanne and Genevieve Perreau of *Figaro* were there. They were all about to witness a thrilling and unforgettable moment in fashion history.

The room was now full to bursting, the stage set, the audience seated and the animated chatter subsiding. Christian Dior was secreted away behind the curtain in the models' cabine with two of his close associates (or 'mothers' as Dior referred to them). Mme Marguerite and the stylish Mme Bricard now gave the sign to start. Mme Raymonde, his right-hand and most trusted colleague, went boldly out front.

Ernestine Carter of *Harper's Bazaar* described the event:

"The model girls entered the salon, their tiny hats by Maud et Nano tipped to one side, held on by veils caught under the chin, or else simply defying gravity. As Chanel had invented a stance, Dior had invented a walk, perilously back tilted, which added to the arrogance with which the mannequins pirouetted in their calf-grazing, voluminous skirts (one contained a staggering eighty yards of fabric). It was not only the length (a foot from the ground) that excited; it was the contrast of the discipline of the little bodices with their tiny wasp waists and the billowing grace of the full skirts, the softly curved shoulders and the nonchalant back-dipping, open collars".[1]

Another witness to that first collection was Carmen Baron, who ran Dior's accessories studio. She said, "The flower woman was born; with his fine shoes, and tambourine hats, fake diamonds, veils, small waists, wide hips, Dior had made woman sacred."

These new, feminine silhouettes were voluptuous, extravagant, and irresistible. An elegant afternoon dress named *Corolla*, in fine black wool, was intensely feminine with soft sloping shoulders, buttons to a tiny waist, and a cascade of full, luxurious pleats to accentuate the hips – with the hemline dropped by a dramatic nine inches. A tailored suit called Bar, now considered the iconic New Look ensemble, combined a curvy jacket in a natural shade of shantung silk, softly rounded at the shoulders, with a high bustline tapering into a tiny waist, then curving away from the body out to full-blown hips; and a shockingly full pleated black wool skirt. All 20 yards of it swirled and swished arrogantly as the models sashayed around the room. The price was an astounding FF 59,000 (the average annual wage at this time was about a third of that figure!). The equivalent price would have been €9,000 (£7,500/$12,000).

Ernestine Carter recalled, "The traditional applause for the wedding dress which signals the end of each couture collection swelled into an ovation, some of the audience were in tears and were calling for the designer who was routed out and coaxed through the grey satin curtains to receive the cheers of the press, the kisses of friends and the bursting of flashbulbs."[2]

In Dior's own words, "Mme Marguerite, Mme Bricard and I stood gazing at each other in the dressing room. We were none of us able to speak. Then Mme Raymonde came to look for us, crying with joy, in order to propel us into the big salon where we were greeted to a salvo of applause. As long as I live, whatever triumphs I win, nothing will ever exceed my feelings at that supreme moment".[3]

British fashion designer, John Cavanagh, who was a friend of Dior and was assisting Pierre Balmain in Paris at the time, was transfixed, in tears. "The relief was overwhelming; that relief of seeing total beauty again, from the tips of the little shoes to the feathers on the hats – it was total glorification of the female form," he said.[4]

That collection went down in history as the 'New Look' the moment the editor-in-chief of *Harper's Bazaar*, Carmel Snow, declared, "It is quite a revolution, dear Christian. Your dresses have such a new look."

Ten years after the launch, *Time* magazine summed it up: "Christian Dior had seized the moment. At the end of the war, French haute

RIGHT A summer 1947 black silk evening skirt with linen jacket lavishly embroidered with gold and diamonds by Christian Dior.

LEFT Portrait of Christian Dior by Cecil Beaton, 1954. From the private collection of Mr. Ian Thomas L.V.O.

couture was in the dangerous doldrums. New York was claiming to have supplanted Paris as the wellspring of fashion, so it happened, on that cold winter's day in February 1947 Christian Dior had, remarkably, and in one masterful stroke, reinstated the prominence of French couture, captivating the world and making his name known overnight".[5]

Today, it is hard to imagine what a furor was caused by the New Look, but it electrified fashion. Dior became a household name and the most influential fashion designer of the late 1940s and 1950s, along with his rival, Cristóbal Balenciaga. Although very different, these two designers unleashed a hunger for fashion that had been pent up through the shortages and deprivations of the war years, not only reviving the couture, but initiating what would become a global fascination with fashion as a force in contemporary life.

1 The Revival of French Couture

Until the beginning of the Second World War, the couturiers of the Chambre Syndicale de la Couture Parisienne, founded in the mid-19th century, dominated fashion; and in 1939 there were 70 haute couture salons, including Chanel, Schiaparelli, Vionnet, Dessès, Fath, Lanvin, Lelong, Rochas, Ricci, Patou, Piguet, the American Mainbocher, and the Britain Molyneux. These were centralised in the Golden Triangle of the city's 8th Arrondissement, between the Avenues des Champs-Èlysées, George V and Montaigne.

At the same time, London had its court dressmaker, Norman Hartnell, and in America the glamorous designs of Hollywood films, created by designers such as Gilbert Adrian and Edith Head, were all the rage. Each season the buyers and reporters from the US flocked to the Paris collections to buy and copy.

OPPOSITE A fine wool crepe ball dress, strapless with daring plunge neckline and sweeping back detail. From the Christian Dior *Mid-century* collection of autumn/ winter 1949.

RIGHT A luxurious plum wool coat with deep collar, worn dramatically with jaguar print cloche hat and tote bag originally designed in 1949 by American designer, Pauline Trigère.

THE EFFECTS OF THE SECOND WORLD WAR

The outbreak of WWII changed everything. The Paris couture was cut off from its export customers, the American buyers and the press. With the German occupation of Paris, many fashion houses closed, including Chanel and Vionnet; Molyneux fled to London, while Mainbocher relocated to New York. The Nazis seized the archives of the Chambre Syndicale de la Couture, Jews were excluded from the fashion industry, and the Germans considered relocating the haute couture to Berlin or Vienna.

In Britain and the US, the governments coped with wartime shortages by regulating the amount and types of materials to be used in fashion apparel. Silk and wool fabrics were replaced by rayon and wool blended with synthetics. Zippers were prohibited to preserve metal, while rubber was in short supply, resulting in dress styles that did not require girdles or shapely underpinnings.

While fashion continued in Paris, the Chambre Syndicale was also limited; four metres of cloth were permitted for a coat, and only one metre for a blouse, and inferior materials were substituted. French creativity found an outlet in extravagant hats, which were often made from scraps of leftover materials.

Although shortages and rationing continued after the war, particularly in Britain, in liberated Paris the couture was quickly revived. Not only were Parisian women anxious to wear pretty things again; the revival of the French couture was a business necessity. The emergence of a strong American fashion business, driven

OPPOSITE A smart, slim-line 1941 wartime costume featuring separate pockets (to save on fabric) in check tweed by Paris house, Pacquin.

ABOVE A 1945 young look by American designer Norman Norell. Fitted waistcoat, collarless shirt, A-line skirt and modern flat sling-back pumps - but check out the formal white gloves.

by ready-to-wear and spawned by 'the American look' of designers Claire McCardell, Norman Norell, Mainbocher, Adrian Gilbert, Charles James and émigré Pauline Trigère, was beginning to threaten France's traditional dominance of fashion.

DIOR AND THE RETURN OF COUTURE

Against this backdrop, Christian Dior's New Look was a brilliant coup. A deliberate display of extravagance, ignoring the practical realities of life, it was never Dior's intention to provide for the masses; but what he did provide

was a spectacle for an entire society. Until 1945, 'glamour' for Europeans meant 'uniform', but the monotony of brown serge and little knee-length dresses with square shoulders had a limited appeal.

Bill Blass, the American designer, reminisced in American *Vogue* in 1999: "You just can't imagine the difference between New York and Paris then. Women in America, no matter how rich, all wore these black rayon crepe dresses because the war restrictions limited you to something like two-and-a-half yards of fabric. So, after years of that, to suddenly see the opulent clothes in Paris, well, it was just sort of

BELOW A simple to sew dress pattern in the style of Dior, found in *Good Housekeeping* magazine dated June 1949.

OPPOSITE British ready-to-wear firm Dereta lost no time replicating the Dior look. This advertisement from May 1949 shows an elegant two-piece suit made in smart barathea with all the latest details.

simple to sew

Make this graceful evening frock, in sleeved or sleeveless design, without sending for a pattern

THIS dress, designed with a full, straight skirt, and bodice seamed down the front with a buttoned fastening down the back, takes 5½ yards of 36-inch material.

You need a pattern only for the bodice, as the skirt consists simply of three panels, each made of a complete width of the material cut to the required length plus at least two inches hem allowance. These are seamed together, and two of the seams arranged in the front of the dress, equidistant from the centre and corresponding to the double balance mark shown on the diagram at the waist of the bodice. The third seam comes at the centre back, and is left open for six inches at the top to form a placket opening.

The waistband is made of a straight strip, nine inches by 25, with the selvedge grain running downward.

To make a pattern for the bodice, study our diagrams carefully. For the long-sleeved dress follow the black outline; for the short-sleeved take the alternate line shown in red. Our diagrams are drawn to scale for a frock with a 25-inch waist and a 34-inch bust. Check your own measurements, and if these do not correspond, modify waist, sleeve and depth of bodice measurements accordingly.

Cut your pattern in paper, lay this on your material, but when you cut out be sure to allow half-inch turnings on all seams, on neckline and on end of sleeves. Make up bodice, matching letters and figures. Stitch the darts, then cut up the fold and press flat. Slash turnings on underarm seams to prevent puckering where seams curve. Face neckline carefully to prevent stretching. Note that a two-inch turning is allowed at centre back for facings, and that the two sides overlap a half-inch to allow for buttoning.

Gather skirt at waist and stitch on to a one-inch petersham. Join to bodice.

Gather waistband at both ends to a width of three inches. Neaten with a facing and fasten with hooks and eyes.

for May 1949

19

deréta

It's sleek, it's simple, it's sophisticated—
a suit for the woman who is sure of herself.
deréta make it in barathea, with
curving pockets to stress a curving hip line,
winged cuffs to flatter your hands and
a straight skirt, very much of this season.

Enquiries to *deréta* (wholesale only)   KENT HOUSE, MARKET PLACE, LONDON, W.1

'This is rich. Screw you.'" For those who could afford it, one of the joys of peace was a return to out-and-out luxury, and in this Christian Dior led the way.

Dior's couture house was inundated with orders. Rita Hayworth chose an evening gown for the premiere of the new film, *Gilda*. Margot Fonteyn bought a suit and it would not be long before European royalty became enthusiastic

clients. Princess Margaret, who had immense charm and style and was widely copied as a young woman, lost no time adding the required length to all of her skirts. She was to become one of Dior's favourite clients.

For those living in grey post-war England, the New Look was as good as it gets. The fact that food rationing dragged on until 1954 and it would take at least a whole year's coupons to buy just one Dior dress was incidental. The style was commercial, and if you could afford the fabric, easy to copy. Magazines like British *Vogue* were sympathetic to their readers, giving plenty of editorial advice on how best to replicate the look on a limited budget and providing access to their easy-to-follow dressmaking patterns.

Ready-to-wear firms soon began a healthy business creating similar, more affordable styles. One such British firm, Dereta, took a chance right away and made up a New Look suit, which flew off the rails of a West End store within two weeks. Harrods also had a franchising arrangement to sell semi-couture from patterns supplied by the Dior workrooms that were immensely popular with debutantes.

The collection was a vision of elegance – new, confident, and unashamedly feminine. Although bodices were boned, hips padded and petticoats worn to make the skirts flare out from the waist like an opened flower, the feeling was of easy, graceful movement. Dior's was the art that concealed, emphasising the bust, hips and ankles and producing newly sensuous erogenous zones. The fashion journalists were simply mad about the look.

Dior's choice of luxurious, closely-woven materials such as duchess satin, taffeta, ottoman, wool crepe and velvet were a feast for the senses, especially after the limp and flimsy wartime utility fabrics; nevertheless the clothes were cut and balanced in such a way that they retained a magical lightness to wear.

Dior was inspired by the genteel toilettes of the Belle Époque, literally translated as 'The Beautiful Era', along with his strong fascination with flowers, their form, shapes and evolvement. He implemented some of the old methods and tricks of corsetry from that bygone era and

re-created his idea of a perfect body, adjusting the amount of underpinning needed for each individual client.

Head of Dior's workrooms, Mme Marguerite, describes the construction of a couture gown from the early fifties: "The tulle scaffolding was put under the dress itself. First the famous No. 132 tulle from Brivet, then a very sheer organza from Abraham to prevent the tulle from scratching and making ladders in the stockings, a very fine silk pongee added to line the skirt. Then there were the tulle corsets made to give them the shape we wished them to have."[1]

OPPOSITE An utterly feminine black wool crepe cocktail dress called *Maxims*, with low décolletage, puffed out skirt and bow at the bodice, from Dior's 1947 debut New Look collection.

RIGHT Boned underpinnings were essential to retain the desired 'hour-glass' figure fifties clothes demanded. A Dior couture dress would have one incorporated within the structure. This 1954 strapless boned corselette, however, is a pretty example and may well be worn on its own as a dress today.

Not everyone was happy about the extravagant new looks, and women complained about the excessive amounts of fabric, corset and padding required. A dress was literally ripped off one of Dior's models while being photographed on the Rue Lepic one afternoon in Paris by an angry housewife. English tailors protested against the length of his skirts and in the United States there were picket lines and even a radio debate about it.

In spite of the protests, Dior offered not merely a new look but a new outlook to fashion. He said, "As a result of the war and uniforms, women still looked and dressed like Amazons. But I designed clothes for flower-like women, with rounded shoulders, full feminine busts, and hand-span waists above enormous spreading skirts."[2]

DIOR'S EARLY LIFE

Christian Dior was born on January 12, 1905 in Granville, a popular seaside town on the Normandy coast. His parents came from some of France's oldest and richest bourgeois families; an uncle was Minister of the Interior under Poincare. Dior learnt to love flowers from his mother (it was his job to decorate the dining-room table when guests arrived for dinner), and as a child he took a delight in designing costumes for his playmates and in

LEFT Women picketing outside Christian Dior's hotel in September 1947 in Chicago, protesting his designs for the New Look longer length skirts.

organising fancy dress parties. When he was ten he drew reprimands from his teachers for his habit of drawing a woman's leg in a high-heeled shoe on his books, examination papers and worksheets.

At 14, Christian had his palm read by a fortune-teller who told him that he would make his living from women and therein lay his future success. His family laughed, moved to Paris in 1910 and attempted to train him to be a diplomat. Dior attended the École des Sciences Politiques. But instead of following the diplomatic life, Dior plunged into the arty life of Paris in the '20s. Velvet-collared, bowler-hatted and rich, Christian hobnobbed with musicians such as Poulenc and Satie, and artists like Jean Cocteau, Christian Berard and Salvador Dali.

Following the death of his mother and the collapse of the family firm, Dior's health suffered and he went south to recover from a lung ailment, returning to Paris in 1935 with no money, but (bizarrely) a new interest in embroidery, which he had learned while convalescing in Majorca. A friend taught him to make fashion sketches, and, to Dior's astonishment, he succeeded in selling them to a fashion house for 120 francs a piece. He worked successively for Robert Piguet and Lucien Lelong as a designer. At Lelong he met Madame Raymonde who later became his

closest collaborator and was in charge of his studio.

After a year's service in the army during the war, Dior was sent to Marcel Boussac, France's biggest owner of textile mills, who was searching for a new designer to inject fresh vitality into Paris' sluggish salons. Boussac listened to Dior's theory that the public was ready for a new style after the war; a luxurious new look with an extravagant silhouette and billowing skirts. As a man who owed his wealth to selling large quantities of luxurious fabric, Boussac did not hesitate to launch the new couture house in style with a then-unprecedented budget of FF 60 million (€9.15 million/£7.6 million/$12.1 million).

In his memoirs Dior recalled, "At Piguet or Lelong I was only a designer; I vanished from sight once my dresses had been created. Once my task was accomplished, I was off to enjoy peace and quiet in the country, and relax after the turbulence of preparing the collection." Dior could not decide whether to stay in his comfort zone at Lelong or to accept Marcel Boussac's offer to start a new house, and turned to another fortune-teller recommended by his friend Mme Raymonde. Reportedly, when the fortune-teller was shown a piece of paper on which he had scribbled a few meaningless sentences, she went into raptures and predicted that it would revolutionise fashion.

BALENCIAGA

Cristóbal Balenciaga was Dior's only serious rival during his ten-year reign over Paris haute couture. While Christian Dior certainly became a legend in his lifetime, Balenciaga is regarded as the architect of post-war fashion. Indeed, even Dior called him the Master, but many of his French rivals referred to him simply as the Spaniard.

Balenciaga had already managed three fashion houses in Spain under the name of his mother, Eisa, when he arrived in Paris in 1937. His first collection reflected the influence of the Spanish Renaissance. As early as 1938 *Harper's Bazaar* were praising the divine blackness of his little black dresses. They described them as, "fitting the figure like a wet glove, unrelieved by any soothing touches, immaculately plain from neck to hem...the black is so black that it hits you like a blow. Thick Spanish black almost velvety, a night without stars, which makes the ordinary black look almost grey."[3]

Although France had become Balenciaga's base, the cultural references that inspired him always came from his Basque country origins and devout religious beliefs. Diana Vreeland knew him well and noted, "He remained forever a Spaniard...His inspiration came from the bullrings, the flamenco dancers, the fishermen in their boots and loose blouses, the glories of the church and the cool of the cloisters. He took the colours, their cuts, then festooned them to his own taste."[4] The carnation, the natural flower of Spain, for example, is woven into the warp and weft of his fabrics and embroidered onto his majestic ball gowns.

His dramatic pleated sleeve coat (winter 1950) recalls the robes of Saint Francis painted by Zurbaran and El Greco. Balenciaga was strongly influenced by Spanish painting; particularly by the work of Velazquez, Goya and Zurbaran. This can be seen in his colours and his use of rich ornament such as black lace, black ball fringe, jet or bead passementerie.

By 1939 Balenciaga had few rivals and was highly praised by his clients and thought of by the French press as a revolutionising force in fashion, always pushing his craft to the limits of creativity with buyers and customers fighting to gain access to his collections. During World War II clients even risked travel to Europe for

OPPOSITE The perfect Paris suit, designed by Balenciaga in 1950. Immaculately tailored with button detail emphasising the waist with narrow mid-calf skirt.

BELOW A detail from a silk evening coat by Balenciaga, intricately embroidered with Melanex, chenille, beads and feathers in vibrant cerise.

his designs, especially the celebrated 'square' coat – in which the sleeves were cut in one piece with the yoke; and for his signature colour combination of black and brown or black lace over bright pink.[5]

It is impossible to guess what he thought of Christian Dior's sudden precedence on that fateful day of the New Look because Balenciaga loathed publicity, never appeared in his salon, was seldom photographed, and, except for his perfumes, refused to have anything to do with commercial exploitation. He disliked the press and the only interview he ever gave was with Prudence Glynn of the *Times*, in August 1971, after his retirement; even then, he diplomatically avoided any professional criticism.

Balenciaga was never a member of the Chambre Syndicale, refusing to participate in the politics and media hype of the French fashion system. As a result, his contributions to fashion were not so well publicised. Later in his career, Balenciaga refused to show his collection until the day before the retail delivery date, rather than the standard four weeks before. Hoping to curtail copying of his designs, he made it nearly impossible for the press to review his show.

Balenciaga designed 400 or so looks a year, somewhat fewer than most other couture houses and about half the number produced

RIGHT Reflecting a continuing return to ecclesiastical shapes, Balenciaga's sweeping statement of a cape and evening gown with graduated hem in silk gazar by Abraham.

OPPOSITE Retaining nostalgia for his native Spain, these early 1950s Balenciaga dresses echo the spirit and seductive movement of flamenco dancers.

by the more commercially aggressive Dior. His shows were totally opposite to Dior's, lasting several hours and conducted in complete silence by frighteningly serious models. Balenciaga only designed for clients who had been personally introduced to him; one could not walk in off the street and commission a dress.

Despite the strict rules and regulations of the house, he had many loyal and wealthy clients including the Duchess of Windsor, Pauline de Rothschild and Mona Bismarck. Carmel Snow was also a favoured customer and became one of Balenciaga's few close friends despite his lack of English, which he never really mastered.

For Carmel Snow he designed the much-imitated stand-away collar to disguise her short neck.

"Balenciaga worked for near fifty years in fashion, so he witnessed dramatic changes in the lives of many of the women he dressed," says Lesley Miller, senior curator of textiles at the V&A, in *Vanity Fair*. "His clothes and innovations reflected his empathy for women's needs and their figures – and how they matured. It is no coincidence that several of his role models were women such as Coco Chanel and Madeleine Vionnet, who also thought about the female body in distinctive ways. While the signpost styles for which Balenciaga gained

his reputation appear to skim the body rather than to hug it, some had built-in foundations or would have been worn over quite substantial underwear. Photographs of his workshop in the 1960s, when underwear was becoming skimpier, show models wearing what are still quite substantial foundation garments under the loose shapes then fashionable."[6]

Diana Vreeland once declared, "If a woman came into a room wearing a Balenciaga dress no other woman existed. He didn't care a bit about youth. He didn't care about bones or anything we admire today. He would often say women did not have to be perfect or beautiful to wear his clothes. When they wore his clothes they became beautiful."[7]

More than 60 years on, *Harper's Bazaar's* extraordinary claim that "almost every woman, directly or indirectly, has worn a Balenciaga," continues to be relevant today as we see his pure lines and perfect proportions displayed on the runways of contemporary designers.

BALENCIAGA'S EARLY INFLUENCES

Cristóbal Balenciaga was born on 21 January, 1895, in the medieval fishing village of Guetaria, in the Basque province of Guipuzkoa, on Spain's rather stormy Cantabrian coast. His father was the captain of a small pleasure boat used during the summer vacations for ferrying King Alfonso XIII and his British born queen, Victoria Eugenia, to the royal yacht.

After his father's death, when Balenciaga was ten, his mother supported the family through her work as a seamstress for wealthy local families. Working beside his mother, Balenciaga was in a good position to observe

OPPOSITE Legendary *Harper's Bazaar* editor Carmel Snow became close friends with Balenciaga who first designed his ubiquitous stand-away collar to disguise Snow's short neck.

ABOVE Balenciaga experimented with baby doll shapes in the mid-fifties. A black lace over-dress with signature bows moves freely while a close-fitting sheath dress hugs the body underneath.

and appreciate beautiful clothing and to learn
the skills that enhanced them from his mother.
He also had connections to royal patronage.

As a boy of about 11, Balenciaga
approached an elegant lady walking along the
street who was wearing an ankle-length costume
of light tussore silk and a straw hat enveloped
in a maroon veil that tied under her chin in a
bow. Balenciaga plucked up enough courage
to stop her and ask if she would let him design
an outfit for her. "Why do you want to do that?"
she asked. He replied directly: "Because I think
I could."[8]

The lady in question was the Marquesa de
Casa Torres. She allowed Balenciaga access
to her wardrobe and entrusted him with the
task of copying one of her Drecoll suits. During
a trip to Paris he visited the houses of Doucet,
Drecoll and Worth, where he was transfixed.
He returned to Spain knowing that his object in
life was to become a great couturier.

He was at first apprenticed to a tailor in
San Sebastian, which included instruction in
many variations of ecclesiastical vestments,
bishop's mantels, clerical cloaks and soutanes
whose shapes are based on simple t-shapes
and circles; these eventually inspired his linear
silhouettes. Later, at 17, he spent several months
in Bordeaux perfecting his French, the language
of his chosen métier.

For six years Balenciaga worked for
Mademoiselle Victoria, in a shop known as
the 'Louvre' in the Calle de Hernani, San
Sebastian, which had become a fashionable
Mediterranean seaside resort, frequented by
the royal family. In 1919 he opened his first

salon bearing his own name in partnership with sisters named Lizasso. At 21 years old he was dressing Queen Victoria Eugenia, the Queen Mother Maria Cristina and their ladies-in-waiting. Along with his tailor, Tomaz Ruez, he would go in person to the Miramar Palace to carry out fittings.

The fall of Alfonso XIII in 1931 put an end to his business, and with the loss of high-ranking clients the house was forced into bankruptcy. However, Balenciaga soon opened another establishment enthusiastically encouraged by his close friend Vladzio d'Attainville (real name Gaborowski), who was the son of one of his clients. This elegant young man of Russian extraction was a little younger than Balenciaga and passionately fond of art and antiquity. He was instrumental in encouraging Balenciaga to widen his artistic horizons.[9]

The new house was situated in Calle Caballero de Gracia in San Sebastian and renamed Eisa after his mother. Spanish law forbade the use of a name associated with bankruptcy so he could no longer use his own name in his native country. Two more fashion businesses were established in Spain under the Eisa name, one in Madrid and another in Barcelona, and were eventually managed by members of the Balenciaga family. They remained open until he retired in 1968.

However, Spain's political upheavals continued to unsettle Balenciaga's life. Fleeing the Spanish Civil War that began in 1936, he first went to London. He admired British tailoring and the tradition of court dressmaking that echoed his own experiences in Spain, but after

OPPOSITE An early Drecoll model in white silk lavishly trimmed in fur; accessorised with a draped silk hat with egret feather trim.

ABOVE Norman Hartnell, favourite couturier of English Royal ladies, was in great demand by debutantes during 'The Season'.

approaching the most prominent of the court dressmakers, Norman Hartnell, and (curiously) the Selfridge department store, he was unable to find a suitable position. He then turned his sights to Paris, where his friend Vladzio d'Attainville's mother lived.

Balenciaga was no stranger to Paris when he decided to set up business there, in fact, he knew it very well. He had been on regular buying trips throughout the 1920s and 1930s where he bought couture models to adapt for the Spanish market. He got to know Madeleine Vionnet quite well; she encouraged him to start work on his own ideas, and they remained friends throughout his long career.

Mainbocher was another designer Balenciaga admired and bought from in the early days, before the Chicago-born designer returned to America. Louise Boulanger, Cheruit, Lanvin, Augusta Bernard, Chanel and Elsa Schiaparelli were all on his list of admired designers from whom he bought at this time. In fact the work of all the great names of the period were absorbed and honed into Balenciaga's artistic conscious.

RIGHT A halter neck yellow silk satin evening dress embroidered with silver; designed by Mainbocher in the late thirties.

OPPOSITE A typical 1940s Schiaparelli print dress in black silk crepe, printed with tiny green shuttered windows, and jaunty straw hat.

Schiaparelli became one of his clients when he opened in Paris, as did Madeleine Vionnet, who was still wearing Balenciaga at the age of 92. In 1967 she was pleased to reveal publicly that she was "happiest in a quilted trouser suit in pink printed silk, and a long camel-hair robe de chambre made by the master."

THE GOLDEN TRIANGLE

Balenciaga borrowed FF 100,000 (€15,245/£12,730/$20,300) from his fellow émigré and silent business partner, Nicholas Bizcarrondo, to open the house of Balenciaga in 1937. He chose the fourth floor of a fashionable apartment building at number 10 Avenue George V in the heart of the Golden Triangle, the area of Paris given over to the luxury trades since the late 19th century.[10]

Balenciaga's salon was located next door to Mainbocher, who dressed practically all the so-called 'Café Society' in his expensive, elegant and understated style before the war. Mainbocher's luxurious designs were chosen by the Duchess of Windsor for her wedding dress and trousseau and he is credited with innovations such as the short evening dress; the famous beaded evening sweaters; the strapless evening gown; sleeveless blouses for suits; the waist cinch; man-tailored dinner suits; bows instead of hats; sari-style evening dress; and many of the looks we continue to wear today.

RIGHT The much-loved trouser suit Cristóbal Balenciaga made for Madeleine Vionnet in 1966 and that she wore into her nineties, made from pink basket weave Matalasse.

OPPOSITE A glamorous 1940s crimson satin evening gown with slim front, flowing back and a matching cape with sable collar and squirrel lining dyed to match the sable, by Mainbocher.

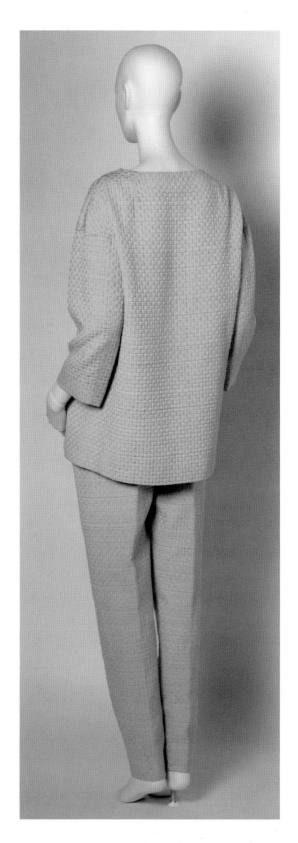

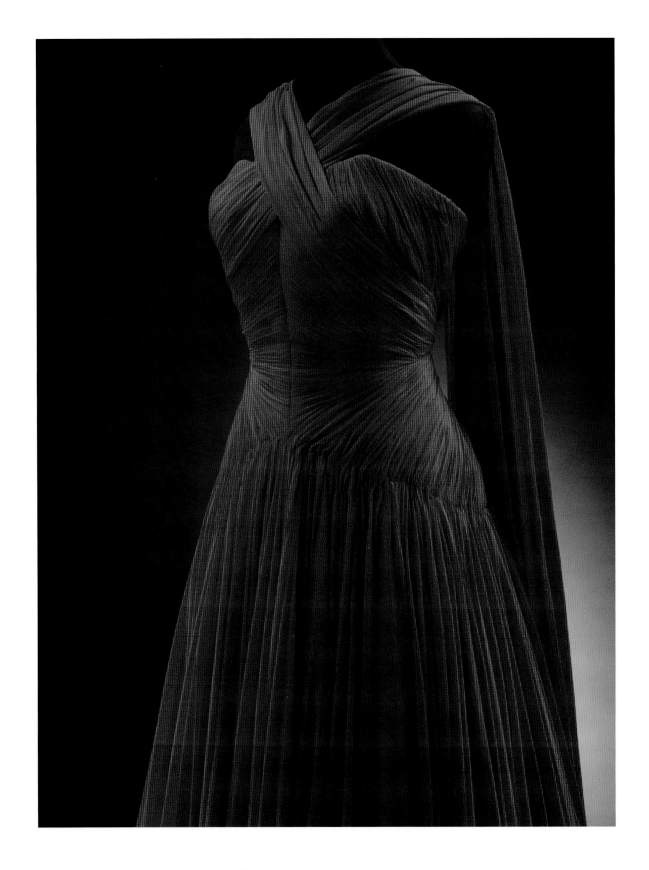

Jean Dessès opened in the same year at number 37. Born in Egypt, to Greek parents, he was known for his beautifully draped chiffon evening gowns, embroidered dresses and sheath dresses with tight jackets. His fashions were popular with European royalty and movie stars.

Jacques Fath, the glamorous self-taught designer who learned his craft from studying museum collections and books about fashion, presented his first collection in 1937, and later relocated nearby in Avenue Pierre 1er de Serbie. During the war he designed "long, fluttering skirts" so that women could ride bicycles during gasoline rationing.

These were the illustrious couturiers Balenciaga set out to challenge in the following years. In 1946, ten years later, Christian Dior opened a little further west and just outside of the triangle, in Avenue Montaigne. As Percy Savage, who designed silk scarves for Balenciaga in the 1960s noted, "Despite the differences in personalities of Dior and Balenciaga, there were, perhaps inevitably, similarities in their designs. Over the years, both showed bloused jackets, both slimmed skirts. Both showed tightly belted fitted jackets, stiffened out into a curve below the waist."[11]

OPPOSITE Jean Dessès dresses are as much sought after for red carpet events today as they were when they were first created in the 1950s.

ABOVE A 1952 Jacques Fath summer dress in gold silk with a flattering deep plunge neckline, tiny waist and full skirt; the hem and sash are in a deeper tone.

THE IMPACT OF THE NEW LOOK

Some would argue that there was nothing new about Dior's New Look. Before the war both Mainbocher and Hardy Amies for Lachasse had shown cinched-in waists. Mainbocher's corset, introduced in his last Paris collection and immortalized in Horst's 1939 photos, caused

LEFT Christian Dior's 1950 fitted suit. The jacket with interest at the front featuring a horseshoe neckline, the skirt consists of two petal-shaped pieces wrapped over each other.

ABOVE A similar 1950 silhouette by Balenciaga. This costume shows a fingertip length jacket in a pile cloth, a camel colour belted tightly at the waist, with pencil slim skirt.

a furor in France and presaged the change in silhouette. Balenciaga had unveiled longer skirt lengths in Paris the year before Dior's New Look; and Pierre Balmain, who had worked with Dior at the House of Lelong, presented a feminine silhouette with long skirts, high bustline, narrow shoulders and small waist in his own first collection in 1945.

Amies, the talented British couturier who later opened his own house in 1946 in London's Savile Row and was soon commissioned to dress the royal princesses, Margaret and Elizabeth and said, "I had felt then, like so many designers, elated by Dior's famous collections. It had shocked some people, but not us. All I could say at the time was, 'Of course, that's how it should be.' For the collection I had launched at Lachasse in the spring of 1939, inappropriate as it seemed for a season that was but the prologue to a terrible war, I had sent girls out to start the collection in tiny corsets. There was to me a feeling in the fashion world of a romantic revival around the corner. In my first post-war collection in the spring of 1946 I had taken up matters where they had been left in 1939. I had not dared to narrow shoulders, nor had I thought of lengthening skirts. In fact, I am sure that without the authority of a French house like Dior, it would not have been possible to change so much in one collection."[12]

LEFT A chic 1951 suit by Hardy Amies in iron-grey wool ottoman. The jacket with feature buttons and flapped hip pockets, accessorised with a mink stole and black patent leather hat by Erik.

2 Post-war Paris and the Business of Couture

As if making up for lost time, post-war Paris was experiencing a great social revival reminiscent of the 'Bright Young Things' antics in the twenties. Everybody who was anybody wanted to give a ball for a particular work, or for his or her friends. In Paris, in the country, on the Eiffel Tower, on a boat on the Seine, in Venice, anywhere where it was a novelty to dance and to dress up. And in Britain, 'the season,' that great marriage market, was revived; presentations at court were reinstated and it became a top priority for fashionable young women to 'come out' in the season's latest white ball gown. Fashion recaptured an aura of luxury and glamour, and couturiers shed the status of 'trade' to become personalities, envied and courted, and in some cases viewed as true artists and style gurus.

As high society regrouped, those who could afford it unashamedly chose to wear opulent couture, precious jewels and furs that bore nostalgic echoes of the Belle Époque. Women, who now had the vote, could fly a plane or drive their own cars, and who in the 1930s had celebrated their progress, now seemed happy to take a more passive, decorative role.

OPPOSITE From left to right, Edward Molyneux's mushroom silk foulard summer suit with white spots and Hardy Amies lavender surah silk dress patterned with pink and white and worn with a cartwheel hat by Erik.

RIGHT A loosely sashed scarlet silk crepe evening gown with cowl neckline and flared sleeves by Madeleine Vionnet.

These highly visible women, through the sheer numbers of their orders and their privileged relationship with the couturiers, were to raise the fashion bar to a status of major art.

THE ART OF FASHION

International fashion reporters, department store buyers and manufacturers would gather for the bi-annual rite of Paris' *couture* collections. The leading French couturiers at this time were Captain Edward Molyneux, Christian Dior, Jacques Fath, Pierre Balmain and Cristóbal Balenciaga. In London the court dressmakers, Norman Hartnell and Hardy Amies, reigned supreme; while the house of Lachasse, established by Digby Morton in 1928, stood for British tailoring, along with Charles Creed. In the US, Adrian, Norell, Mainbocher and Charles James came to prominence designing for the Hollywood stars of the day, then went on to establish their own houses.

These post-war couturiers were predominantly male. Chanel, the modernist, had retired as war broke out, along with the incomparable Vionnet. Edna Woolman Chase, editor of *Vogue* lamented, "Vionnet was unique and perhaps the only true creator in our time in the art of couture. She had invented a way of cutting, a way of sewing pieces of material together that was infinitely complex, but which once mastered had a scientific purity of line. A true artist in fabric."[1] Elsa Schiaparelli's pre-war influence had greatly diminished and

OPPOSITE A sublimely beautiful chiffon jersey draped dress in pale mauve and white, designed in 1952 by the legendary Madame Grès.

LEFT A loosely sashed scarlet silk crepe evening gown with cowl neckline and flared sleeves, by Madeleine Vionnet.

only Madam Grès continued with her Greek-inspired draping.

At the same time the great fashion magazines such as *Vogue*, *Harper's Bazaar* and, in France, *Le Jardin des modes* and *Elle* encouraged society ladies to dress in haute couture, provoking fierce rivalry among them to be included in the pages of the magazines, or in the annual International Best Dressed list founded by American fashion arbiter Eleanor Lambert in 1940.

American *Vogue* flourished under the art direction of Russian émigré Alexander Liberman whose appreciation of abstract expressionist painting and its connection with jazz music was reflected in the clean-cut layouts and strong graphic images of Irving Penn, Henry Clarke and William Klein's fashion photography.

Rival publication *Harper's Bazaar* had the ground-breaking Russian émigré Alexey Brodovitch who encouraged photographers to

ABOVE Mrs Carmel Snow of *Harper's Bazaar* looks over the magazine's layout with art director Alexey Brodovitch.

OPPOSITE Model Jean Dawnay works in the studio with John French and assistant in London in 1958.

apply pioneering documentary techniques to the recording of style. Throughout his career he revolutionised magazine design with his signature use of white space, his innovation of *Bazaar*'s iconic Didot logo, and the cinematic quality that his obsessive cropping brought to layouts (not even the work of Man Ray or Henri Cartier-Bresson was safe from his busy scissors). With his directive "Astonish me," he inspired some of the greatest visual artists of the 20th century, including protégés Irving Penn, Hiro, and Richard Avedon, to create legendary images.

The success of Dior's feminine silhouette heightened the elegance, income and social standing of models Lisa Fonssagrives, Dorian Leigh, Dovima, Sunny Harnett and Suzy Parker, as captured by photographers Irving Penn, Lillian Bassman, Louise Dahl-Wolfe, Cecil Beaton, Richard Avedon, John Rawlings and John French.

Although photographic images suited the new attitude to fashion, illustration was also at its peak with great artistic talents such as Christian 'Bebe' Berard, Rene Gruau, Carl 'Eric' Erickson, Dagmar, and Cecil Beaton. Never before had fashion been so exciting, newsworthy, and controversial.

THE GROWTH OF DIOR

With the money Dior made from his first collection he was able to fulfill his old ambition of having a house in the country. He retreated to Le Coudret, built solidly in stone with a pretty courtyard on the edge of a river with a rambling garden all the way around, to work on a new collection. The process was long and painstaking, and he began by making tiny sketches: "I scribble everywhere, in bed, in my bath, at meals, in my car, on foot, in the sun, in electric light, by day, and by night. Bed and bath, where one is not conscious, so to speak, of one's body, are particularly favourable to inspiration; here one's spirit is at ease. There is also the element of chance inspiration – stones, trees, human beings, mere gestures, or a sudden ray of light, may all be bearers of little whispered messages."[2]

Dior often embroidered endless variations on a theme; when he saw something emerging, he would make a larger drawing. "The next morning it is the turn of another line – which has perhaps come to me during the night – to give me the signal. Little by little the pile of drawings grows, demanding new treatment capable of exploring all their potentialities. Finally this crazy burst of scribbling comes to an end.

OPPOSITE A softly draped jacket and button - through skirt suit in lightweight woo from spring 1955, from Dior's A Line collection.

Then I behave like a baker who knows when to leave a well-kneaded pastry alone. Now that the line from which the new fashion can emerge is determined, I stop. I examine all my sketches, from the first, which are scarcely more than rough outlines, to the last born, where the shapes are much more clearly defined. I sense from the first what promises well; the worthless element eliminates itself."[3]

Back at the studio he would put his sketches into the hands of Mme Marguerite, who had been brought in from a rival couture house. Her job, to interpret Dior's sketches and turn them into clothes, was vital. He would seat himself at a light table near the window, dressed in his white butcher's coat and brandishing his gold-tipped bamboo cane with which he pointed and criticized, giving orders for a neckline to be lowered, a seam moved or a hem shortened. His three muses, Mme Marguerite, Mme Raymonde and Mme Bricart (his chief stylist, who had previously worked with Molyneux), would be present.

The sketches (*petite gravures*) were passed from hand to hand, while Dior would comment on them and fill in the gaps with the help of a few purely technical explanations about the cut or the lay of the material. Dior himself never learned how to sew or even to cut. His talent lay in finding exactly the right collaborators to execute his designs, and to inspire them fully with the ideas he had in his head. As the most prestigious Paris couture house, Dior attracted the most talented assistants.

Dior's staff was eager to please him and to make the right 'expression' when interpreting his designs. His three collaborators, the Mesdames

ABOVE Christian Dior in 1950, dressed in his habitual crisp white coat and armed with bamboo pointing stick, views a new model shown on a house mannequin. Madame Marguerite, his right-hand assistant, is by his side.

Bricard, Marguerite and Raymonde set the atelier in motion, and under the hawk-like eyes of Dior and the three assistants the collection would be finished within six to seven weeks. Like a theatrical performance, it was a collective art, with many hands working towards the final expression including the artisan flower and button makers, embroiderers and milliners.

In Dior's second collection for autumn/winter 1947, the *Corolla* line became more exaggerated. There was still softness on the shoulders, the waist nipped with skirts full and long, but there was a lighter feel. The new long skirt had a skating look, a swirling, waltzing movement. The back views of the slimmer skirts became more important. In France it was called the 'derriere de Paris'. Not a bustle, not a pouffe, more a seductive exaggeration, it was often built on an arrangement of folded drapery with a skirt caught in below.

As skirts became wider, coats became bulkier, while hats became smaller and neater. Dior's coats were exciting, especially those designed for cocktail and eveningwear. In black wool, a redingote called *Mystere* featured dramatic, finely pleated green taffeta bursting out of the neck as a shawl collar, tapering into a tiny waist and then fanning out as a pleated facing to the ankle-length hem. There were majestically glamorous ball gowns and opera coats, perfect for the new passion for grand balls, dances and opulent dinners amongst the emerging European elite.

The grand centrepiece of the 1947 winter collection was an afternoon dress called *Diorama*; in black wool crepe it had a skirt 40 metres in circumference, requiring 45 yards of material. Unthinkably extravagant under post-war rationing, it was everything women craved, the ultimate in luxury.

Dior was not only an inspired designer, but a savvy businessman; and used publicity and licensing to bring his fashions to a wider public. Dior had had the foresight to employ Harrison Elliot, a bright young American who took care of press and publicity for the company. However, six months after the launch Elliott was doing the work of ten men, and even so could not cope with the extraordinary variety of demands made upon his time by the press.

At this point Dior realised he would need to see its principal representatives personally. He had to learn how to fend off indiscreet questions with a smile, to extend a warm welcome to all the world, appear to be delighted at seeing so many of his designs reproduced and at the same time feel furious if too many were.

Having made the necessary contacts with the press, he had to meet the professional buyers and their backers as well. He knew practically none of them personally, though their names were familiar to him – I Magnin, Hattie Carnegie, Neiman Marcus, Bergdorf Goodman, Bendel and Marshall Field. Dior was mature and urbane enough to endure what must have been a tremendous amount of stress that his instant success had suddenly created.

In September 1947 Dior took his first trip to New York on the *Queen Elizabeth*, continuing on to Dallas, where he received the Neiman Marcus Award for Distinguished Service in the Field of Fashion, created by Stanley Marcus, the store's founder, in 1938. Among the ship's fellow passengers were Alexander and

Tatiana Liberman and Bettina Ballard of US *Vogue*. By the time they reached New York they were firm friends.

Dior could not have hoped for a nicer and more influential group to introduce him to America. Alexander Liberman later made this comment about Dior: "Christian Dior brought elements of the can-can, the bordello, and their frou-frou into fashion. He also had the erotic subconscious of a provincial French bourgeois."

While Dior's visit met with protests, and placards greeted him saying 'Burn Mr. Dior' and 'Down with the New Look', the US trip was highly successful. Even at this early stage of his success, Dior was aware of the changing realities of the fashion business, including the growth of ready-to-wear. The big US stores now only stocked a line of made-to-measure dresses for the sake of prestige — and often at a loss. He knew his company could not hope for the lavish orders which his predecessors Vionnet, Chanel, Schiaparelli and Lanvin had enjoyed from American buyers before the war; but only carefully premeditated orders, limited to the models which were either most typical of the new fashion, or easiest to reproduce.

Jacques Rouet, who was his business partner, had expansive ideas from the start. The old Paris couture houses were small operations making bespoke clothes for private clients; but some couturiers had diversified into other products. For example, Chanel, Schiaparelli and Jean Patou had launched successful perfumes, and Schiaparelli had entered into licensing agreements to manufacture hats, hosiery and sunglasses in America.

Rouet's sights were focused further afield into more products and international markets; and by year's end the House of Dior, backed by Boussac's billions, created a perfume division and launched its first fragrance, *Miss Dior*, with the US market in mind. A fur subsidiary and a luxury ready-to-wear operation with a boutique on New York's Fifth Avenue soon followed, and from 1948 Dior was obliged to combine two roles, that of top couturier in Paris, and that of a designer of luxury ready-to-wear in New York.

The financial success of the Christian Dior Company during the 1950s was a good part

ABOVE Dior adjusts Hollywood star Jane Russell's custom-made dress from the *H* Line collection. September 1954.

OPPOSITE Barbara Golan models a 1947 Dior black satin ball dress decorated with silver fringed beads.

due to the pioneering licensing agreements and ready-to-wear lines Dior and his business partner, Jacques Rouet, astutely set up shortly after the 1947 launch. In early 1949, Dior signed his first licence for the manufacture of stockings and ties by American firms. Later that year the second scent, *Diorama*, was released.

At the end of 1949, Dior's New Look line alone had made a profit of FF 12.7 million (€1.94 million/£1.62 million/$2.58 million). Dior fashions made up 75% of Paris's fashion exports and 5% of France's total revenue. 1950 saw the formation of a wholesale business to distribute accessories produced for the Dior label.

By now Christian Dior's fame and celebrity was so great that gendarmes were called out to control the mob at his Paris openings. Like most of the couture, attendance at Dior's show was by invitation only, and security was tight. Some three hundred people would usually be invited to a Dior show, mostly from the US. The buyers, but not the press, were required to pay a fee to see the collection, which was forfeited if they failed to place an order. Dior was terrified of his designs being stolen, and he once physically ejected a woman who he saw sketching one of his dresses.

Besides dressing many prominent socialites, Dior also realised the importance of Hollywood. He was chosen as the exclusive designer of Marlene Dietrich's dresses in the Alfred Hitchcock film *Stage Fright* (1950). Olivia de Havilland and Jane Russell were also loyal clients.

THE EXPANSION OF BALENCIAGA

While the tailored, feminine silhouette defined by the New Look dominated women's fashion into the early 1950s, Dior was not the only couturier to find success during these years. During the post-war years, Balenciaga's designs became more streamlined and linear, differing markedly from Dior's New Look. He used bold, heavy fabrics such as satin, shantung, ottoman and doubleknit, and ornate embroideries; together with the Swiss fabric house of Abraham he developed silk gazar, a stiff fabric that suited his technique. Rather than using interior support structures and corsetry to underpin his designs, Balenciaga sculpted his garments to drift over the body and flatter the wearer, no matter what her age or figure.[4]

In the early years in Paris only essential staff were employed at Balenciaga. At the top of the ladder were Balenciaga and his two business partners, Vladzio d'Attainville, who designed the hats until his death in 1948, and Nicolas Bizcarrondo. Below them were those who collaborated in the design process, Ramon Esparza, who later took over the designing of the all-important hats, and Fernando Martinez, who helped with many of the models. He was a better illustrator than Balenciaga and produced drawings to Balenciaga's exact specifications. The designers Courrèges and Ungaro worked with Balenciaga in the 1950s as apprentice couturiers, and later went on to establish their own businesses. The directrice, the formidable Renee Tanister, managed the premises.

OPPOSITE With inspiration from Spanish fishermen a dramatic and elegant polka dot print smock, slim skirt and wide brim hat, by Balenciaga.

At a lower level, yet still important in the hierarchy of the house, were the tailors and cutters who brought their work to Balenciaga for approval. On the next rung came employees who were actually involved in the making of the models. The premières d'atelier presided over the workrooms. Balenciaga's cutters were substantially better paid than the premières d'atelier because of the sculptural perfection and deviation from the traditional methods of cut and construction. The seamstresses completed the main behind-the-scenes staff.

Balenciaga also employed people who dealt with the public, ten house mannequins, the vendeuses who attended to individual clients, the window-dresser, the boutique attendant, the receptionist and the doorman. In the back rooms were the mannequin dressers, the storeroom staff and the accounting department.

Balenciaga's innovations were many and his passion for his métier absolute. In 1951 Balenciaga challenged the reigning silhouette by broadening the shoulders and eliminating the waist. He approached his work with as much dedication as a priest, inventing the semi-fitted suit, the chemise, melon sleeves, the balloon skirt, the pillbox hat, the 7⁄8 tunic, the high-waisted suit, the cocoon curve coat, the tunic dress, the sack dress, wide shoulders, panel backs, huge collars, necklines cut high in front and low in back, the baby-doll dress, the wearing of boots with couture and black stockings and was one of the first to use the leotard as part of an outfit.[5]

Balenciaga's creations were fluid and graceful with tailoring that was structured in a uniquely soft and feminine way. He had an advantage over many of his rivals in that he had learnt the skill of an expert tailor and he could also drape, cut, and fit his own muslin patterns.

Although he was against licensing his name, to his financial detriment, Balenciaga did bring out a range of perfumes and accessories. His first scent, *Le Dix*, named after the couture house at 10 Avenue Georges V, was launched in 1948. *La Fruite des heures* (1948) and *Quadrille* (1955) were followed by a range of accessories including scarves and handbags; and three brands of stockings named after his perfumes were launched by T.B. Jones in Britain in September 1960.

There were other top couturiers during these post-war years, each with his champions. A favourite was the young, tall and very handsome Marquis Hubert Taffin de Givenchy, with a title more than four centuries old, whose gambit was daring colours and unusual fabrics. Hubert de Givenchy had created a sensation in 1952 with his *separables*, following the American idea of separates, which could be

RIGHT Balenciaga was a master at understated luxury. A blonde fur coat over simple wool dress looks divine accessorised with a red scrolled hat and glamorous red lipstick.

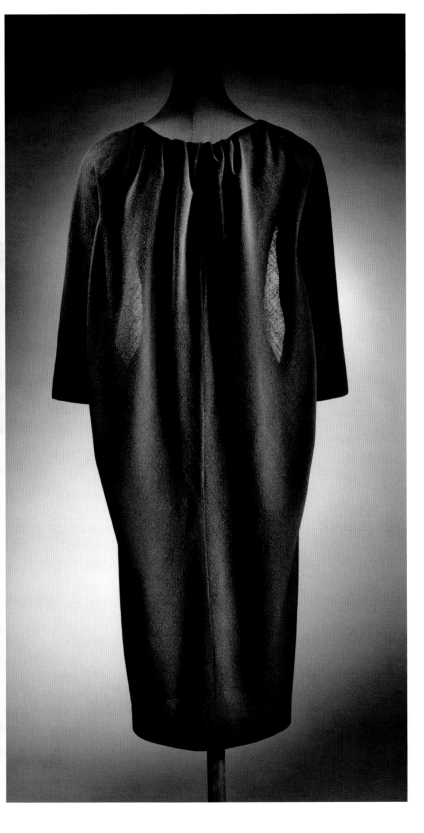

mixed and matched at will (a very new idea in 1950s couture). He shared Balenciaga's concept of designing the perfect, simple dress from a single line; the two met in 1953, and developed a close working relationship.

Givenchy also found Hollywood to be an important source of patronage and a key marketing proposition. His big break came when Balenciaga turned down a request to dress Audrey Hepburn for her fourth film, *Sabrina* (1954), recommending his friend Givenchy, who had just opened in Paris. Hepburn and Givenchy's instant rapport lasted a lifetime and produced many innovative and iconic costumes. The little black dress worn by Hepburn in *Breakfast at Tiffany's* (1961) would have been enough to assure Givenchy's name for posterity.

Pierre Balmain, who had worked for Molyneux as well as Lelong, established his own house in 1945. Known for sophistication and elegance, he popularized the stole for day and the vogue for sheath dresses worn beneath jackets as well as his celebrated grand evening gowns and many costume designs for Hollywood movies. He also made Audrey Hepburn's wedding dress when she married Mel Ferrer in 1954.

Jacques Fath dressed "the chic young Parisienne and Hollywood set." Amongst his clients were the movie stars Rita Hayworth,

OPPOSITE Thick grey wool coat with 'melon' sleeve, tiny stand-up collar and beret-style hat by Balenciaga, 1950.

LEFT Back view of the innovative 1957 Balenciaga sack dress in fine black wool. The front view is gathered into the waist with a bow for maximum versatility.

Ava Gardner, and Greta Garbo; he designed the costumes for Moira Shearer in the 1948 movie *The Red Shoes*. Fath made Rita Hayworth's wedding dress and entire trousseau when she married Prince Ali Khan in 1949. Fath was as famous for his extravagant parties as for his fashion and his wife and muse, Genevieve, his best advertisement, who always looked immaculate by his side. A number of young, soon-to-be successful designers became Fath's assistants – Hubert de Givenchy, Guy

Laroche and Valentino Garavani, who also worked for Balenciaga and Jean Dessès.

Pierre Cardin was the son of Italian farmers who had emigrated to the Loire in 1926. He was apprenticed to a tailor in St. Etienne where he worked until 1944. Cardin then gained a position with Paquin in the Rue de la Paix and went on to become head tailor at Dior, working there during the launch of the New Look. He opened his own costume business in 1949, with the financial support of Dior.

LEFT Audrey Hepburn with husband, Mel Ferrer, at a 1955 Givenchy couture showing in Paris. A typically elegant suit and coat on a Hepburn look-alike model.

OPPOSITE Audrey Hepburn models a little black dress by Givenchy; one of the costumes she wore in the Blake Edwards film *Breakfast at Tiffany's*.

THE AMERICAN LOOK

Couture, in the Parisian sense, scarcely existed in America, although there were seriously good American couturiers, including Mainbocher, Valentina and Charles James, whose designs in the 40s and 50s were like sculptures; and since the war many talented young American designers had emerged.

American ready-to-wear fashion production was ahead of Europe, with basic fabrics like cotton and cotton corduroy easy to source. Manmade fibres such as nylon were also being used in more inventive ways. American women were demanding fashion that was chic, adaptable, affordable and easy to wear. Claire McCardell became the outstanding example

OPPOSITE A grey wool dress, fitted at the waist with feature triangular shaped pockets worn with an angora cloche hat, by Claire McCardell.

RIGHT Tina Leser's 1945 modernist sensibilities are demonstrated here with a hooded plaid coat and Leser's take on the kilt, belted at the waist and trimmed with leather.

of the *American Look* and was one of the first American designers to have name recognition.

As Georgia O'Keeffe once so aptly said, "Parisian fashion carries the perfume of the salon but American style blows in from the great outdoors". McCardell had studied and respected the tools and traditions of French haute couture dressmaking, but by the mid-thirties felt those clothes were too structured, formal and – if copied verbatim – too costly to buy and keep up for busy young women like herself. Like fellow designers Tina Leser, Clare Potter, and Tom Brigance, McCardell and her clients were moving fast into a sophisticated world where women were more than housewives.[6]

In the mid-forties and fifties, Claire McCardell's clean-cut, elegant and above all comfortable clothes designed for Townley Frocks, a New York based, mid-priced dress and sportswear manufacturer, included a six-piece wardrobe of interchangeable separates that were the embodiment of modernism – whether for the beach or a formal dinner. Structures were soft and fluid, and details were kept simple, including devices such as spaghetti ties, bias cut cords for which she seemed to find a million uses. Usually they were tucked just below the bust to give a woman a choice of waistlines, a principle tenet in McCardell's code of fit.

LEFT Claire McCardell started her designs with a sketch rather than draping fabric straight onto the body.

OPPOSITE Two contemporary summer designs in a tablecloth check printed cotton, both designed by Claire McCardell for summer 1946.

Most fashion designers today can thank Claire McCardell for her forward thinking ideas at a time when women were becoming more active in work and leisure. She found much of her inspiration in utilitarian items such as railroad workers double-stitched and riveted work clothes. The workaday bandana kerchief became one of her favourite soft necklines when she stitched its triangular shape to the back of her dresses and knotted it in front. The right-angled pocket flaps of the cowhand's frontier pants turned up on the skirt of a wool suit and the pants themselves were reproduced for girls in pink denim. Another of her fresh, new looks was the pleated bosom and tab collar of custom-made British dress shirts that she adapted to some of her best-selling shirtdresses.

McCardell said that after her number one inspiration – the American woman – came the fabric she would use and what it could do. Her choice of fabric was as down-to-earth as she was, but in unorthodox and often trend-setting ways: wool jersey or cotton for cocktail dresses, tweed or camel's hair for evening wraps, mattress ticking for a town suit, nylon tricot for a dinner dress. Her denim and seersucker cotton wrap-over dresses and dirndl skirts were worn well into the 60s'. She liked flat shoes with her designs and during times of shortages improvised by covering basic ballerina pumps with matching dress material, a fashion still popular today.

McCardell received multiple honours in the 1950s and eventually earned an appearance on the cover of *Time* magazine on May 2, 1955. In 1990 *Life* magazine named her one of the 100 most important Americans of the 20th century.

ITALY ENTERS THE *HAUTE COUTURE*

In 1950 Italy decided to make an entrance into haute couture. While they had been exporting fashion accessories and small leather goods since the early 20th century, and moreover had a strong history of success with luxury textiles, shoes, and jewellery production since the 12th century in Venice, Florence, and Rome respectively, Italy came onto the couture fashion scene quite late. But the historically insecure governmental structure resulted in the absence of a unified Italian fashion centre, thereby estranging the country's fashion artists from competition in the mid-century global market.

In the immediate post-war period, entrepreneur Giovanni Battista Giorgini was employed by American department stores to select and purchase Italian-made products and had the idea of organising a fashion group and a series of fashion shows in his own Florentine residence, the Villa Torriani. It was not until February 1951 that he succeeded in getting the most important American buyers and press to the first fashion show held in Florence, with Carmel Snow, the editor of US *Harper's Bazaar* ,among them.

He decided to showcase a small group of Italian couturiers; many were also aristocrats

OPPOSITE A white silk sari-style evening gown with bead embroidered neckline and floor length coat, by Simonetta et Fabiani.

such as Simonetta Colonna Visconti di Cesaro, Carosa (Princess Giovanna Caracciolo), Maria Antonelli, Alberto Fabiani, Emilio Schubert, Noberasco, Vanna and the Fontana sisters. A fashion boutique and knitwear section was also included, represented by Emilio Pucci, Avolio, Franco Bertoli and Clarette Gallotti.

It was such a resounding success that the next fashion show had to take place at the Pitti Palace. There, in 1952 in the Sala Bianca,

the 19-year-old Roberto Capucci made his debut. This was the birth of the *Italian school*, which began to compete with the French couture. Labels such as Ferragamo, Gucci, and Pucci, whose printed silk jersey shift dress in vivid and unexpected colour juxtapositions that folded flat and small as a handkerchief and emerged perfect from a dozen suitcase journeys, became jet-set essentials and internationally known.

LEFT The flamboyant Roberto Capucci in his 20s studying sketches from a 1958 couture collection.

OPPOSITE White wool coat by Christian Dior from the 1955 A Line collection. Cut narrow at the top with a wing collar, gradually widening at the hip level pockets.

DIOR AND YVES SAINT LAURENT

Despite fashion's international expansion, Dior remained the most sought after couturier throughout his ten-year reign, having built an international clientele including members of the British Royal family, among them Princess Margaret, the Duchess of Devonshire and the Duchess of Marlborough. The first London Dior boutique was established in 1950 at 9 Conduit Street. The same year he staged a fashion show in honour of Princess Margaret and the Duchess of Marlborough at Blenheim Palace; Dior also made the enchanting pale pink organza dress Princess Margaret wore for the Cecil Beaton portrait to commemorate her 21st birthday.

For summer 1953, the year Dior hired Yves Saint Laurent, the *Vivante* (Living) line was launched, a fashion for going out on the street. It suggested a less restricted waistline and shorter skirts. The question of length started another controversy. *Time* magazine noted in August 1953, "Dior mannequins glided into his showroom wearing skirts of startling shortness, their hems raised to a height of 15 to 17 inches above the floor (present average 12 inches)".[7]

Although not as dramatic as the New Look, the *Vivante* line of Autumn/Winter 1953/4 presented a less structured silhouette, coats were collarless and streamlined and the new evening dresses were designed to eliminate the need for boned corseting. His explanation: "How many times have I heard men complain

LEFT Christian Dior directing the workshop staff while working on a new collection, possibly his last, in January 1957.

that, while dancing, they were not able to feel the living body of women under the yoke which imprisoned them?"[8]

A licence was issued for the manufacture of lingerie in 1954; and further branches were set up in Caracas, Australia, Chile, Mexico and Cuba. In 1955 Saint Laurent became Dior's design assistant and the Grand Boutique opened on Avenue Montaigne, the same year

Dior launched a range of cosmetics.

Perhaps inspired by Balenciaga's more linear, less fitted designs, by the mid-fifties the extreme hourglass figure was replaced by a more geometric style. In 1954, Dior's H line dropped the waist to the hip; the next season Dior introduced the A line, narrow at the top, widening lower down. The long jacket persisted, along with the high, gentle bosom,

but the loose waist could come anywhere from just below the breast to low hip level. In 1955 the *Y* line reversed the silhouette, with a new emphasis on the shoulders.

In 1956 *La Ligne Aimant* echoed the liberating softness of Poiret whilst the spring 1957 collection called *Libre* was inspired by the fisherman's smock. Dior's inventiveness knew no bounds; he seemed to renew himself every season, startling and delighting the world of fashion, always providing something new to give the journalists a storyline and to ensure his brand continued to be desirable.

Dior's last collection was for the autumn 1957 season – his tenth year as a *couturier*. He called it the *Fuseau* (Spindle) line. No one knew, of course, that this was to be his finale. Dior's death in October that year was alarmingly sudden. He died of a heart attack after choking on a fishbone while on a rest cure at a spa in Montecatini, Italy.

As fate would have it his last collection was as memorable as his first. The loose, chemise shape Dior had been thinking about for some time had finally materialised. This unfitted dress came to be known as the shimmy, the tube, the sack, the shift. Predictably, like so many of Dior's new ideas, it attracted a good deal of negative criticism. Described at first as shapeless, baggy and inelegant; within months women were wearing it, paving the way for the styles of the 60s by designers such as Mary Quant and André Courrèges.

LEFT A bronze wool cocktail dress threaded with gold, its skirt draped from the hip, shown at Christian Dior's autumn 1956 collection in London.

In November 1957, in accordance to Dior's wishes, Marcel Boussac chose Yves Saint Laurent to replace him as design director. At just 21 years of age, it was now Saint Laurent's turn to impress the world. He had been Dior's assistant for two years, and 30 outfits in Dior's final collection were based on Saint Laurent's own designs. Dior thought the press should be told of his contribution but before anything could be arranged Dior had passed away.

In Saint Laurent's first collection for Dior (spring 1958) he took the *Fuseau* line and the *Libre* line and combined them with the *A* line to make his own, *Trapeze* line. This was hailed in the US as "the first big change in female fashions since the New Look in 1947." The Duchess of Windsor was so impressed she bought the whole collection, and the French newspaper headlines claimed that Saint Laurent had "saved France."

CHANEL RETURNS

In 1954, at the age of 70, Coco Chanel came back into the picture. Her philosophy had not changed: that clothes should be dateless, ageless, relaxed, and, above all, easy to wear. She went out to save womankind from what she called 'fifties horrors.' She showed her famous little untailored braided suit with gold chains, silk blouses in colours that matched the jacket linings, monogrammed gilt buttons, shiny costume jewellery, flat black silk bows, sleek, hand-loomed tweeds, her white fabric camellia, boaters, quilted bags on chains and beige sling back shoes with a darker toe. Hardly different from what she had shown 15 years before. The press were critical, but she had triumphed

once again and her neat, elegant, comfortable and expensive suits were copied all over the world, something she seemed to relish. In what must be the biggest understatement of all fashion time, Chanel said, "I consider myself quite limited in what I do. Therefore it must be meticulous, and the material must be beautiful. As much as possible I must show a little taste and not change too much."[9]

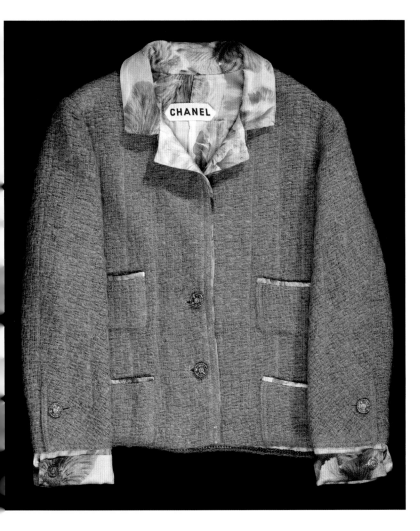

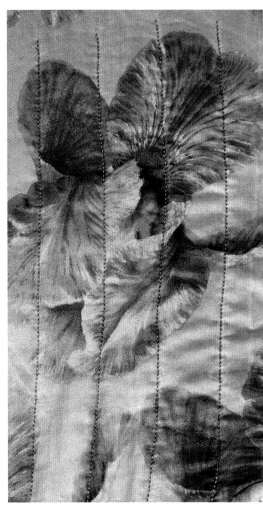

OPPOSITE Gabrielle
Coco Chanel in 1959
with model Suzy Parker
wearing a Prince of
Wales check suit with
lining and over blouse in
Petillaut silk surah.

ABOVE A 1964 model of
a lavender handwoven
wool tweed jacket with
four pockets, French cuffs
and detail showing the
finely padded silk lining,
by Chanel.

Her impeccably made suits may have looked simple from the outside but one of the features that distinguish *couture* from ready-to-wear is the way in which linings are mounted into a garment. Those neat little Chanel suits owe as much to superb tailoring and Chanel's original way of lining the jackets as they do to design. For example, the light mohair and tweed fabrics were fully interlined with silk chiffon, very carefully, and lightly mounted to the fabric to give delicate extra substance. Some linings were quilted with vertical lines of stitching one and a half inches apart. Consequently the jacket would feel as soft as a cardigan and would be easy to move in, but the quilting maintained the shape.

Skirts were fully lined and hand-stitched with pure silk lining. The waistband of a Chanel skirt was also lined with silk. The lining of the jacket droops into a soft pleat at the lower back section, in order to hide a heavy gilt chain. This would be hand-stitched to the top of the hem allowance, and completely concealed by the fall of the silk lining, helping to keep the loose fitting, open-fronted suit jacket in place without riding forward with the wearer's movements.

By 1962 Chanel's coats and suits were the most copied in the Western world, as were her short black velvet and brocade theatre suits. Chanel had steered clear of fashion, which comes and goes; instead she had formulated a *style* and stuck with it. Particularly good copies were made in Britain for Geoffrey Wallis and the chain of Wallis shops. (Here the author freely admits to being the proud owner of one such suit at age 14.)

While Chanel never regained her pre-war domination of the Paris scene, she remains the most famous couturiere of the century. But new talents were crowding in. Of all the newcomers, it was Yves Saint Laurent to whom Chanel was most sympathetic, perhaps flattered because of his admiration of her. She contented herself with saying, as quoted by fashion editor Felicity Green, that "the poor boy might turn out alright if he copied me and cut his hair". It is not known if this was before or after he proved his admiration by dedicating a collection to her – *Homage á Chanel* – in which he did indeed copy her in a different way, repeating her typical mannerisms, even down to the artificial gardenia on the lapel. But he did not cut his hair.

COUTURE MOVES ON

With the loss of Dior, other designers with new ideas began to emerge as strong competition to the house, such as Pierre Cardin, who had been head of Dior's tailoring workroom in 1947.

Cardin opened his own house in 1950, and was later known for his geometric shapes and 'Space Age' designs.

Fashion was moving into the future, and the young and rebellious Saint Laurent countered the challenge with his 1960 *Beat Look* for Dior, inspired by the bikers and students of Paris' Left Bank. The collection was not so well received by the chic women of Paris, who did not want to wear black leather suits, black woolly hats and black turtleneck sweaters. In 1960 Yves Saint Laurent was replaced by Marc Bohan, who had worked at Piguet, Molyneux and Patou before moving to Dior's London branch, and could be relied upon not to frighten the horses.

André Courrèges was a qualified engineer with a passion for architecture when he went to work for Balenciaga, where he remained for 11 years. His former employer also lent him enough money to set up on his own in 1961 and generously sent him a number of clients prepared to try something more adventurous. His geometric shapes, short skirts, and use of bright colours, metal and plastic were a sensation. Courrèges was one of the first of the haute couturiers in Paris to capitalise on mass-producing his own designs, thus avoiding the licensing system.

The fashion zeitgeist now favoured the shapes and structures perfected by the *Master*, Balenciaga. Throughout the 1960s he continued to show collections of unparalleled technique and beauty, with designs often encrusted with exquisite embroidery. His unflinching perfectionism was legendary. "No one in French couture can match him," wrote the *New York Times* in 1967.

ABOVE Marc Bohan, who succeeded Yves Saint Laurent as creative director for Dior, with models and *Glamour* magazine's fashion editor, Ellin Saltzman (wearing clothes from his spring 1964 collection for Dior).

Balenciaga's summer 1968 collection, shown on the eve of Paris's student riots, was, for Pauline de Rothschild (an avid collector of Balenciaga), "the collection of a very young man together with all the knowledge." This statement said it all… that season, at 71, he was showing tiny shorts suits, dresses miraculously cut with a single seam, and dramatic trapezoid evening gowns created from stiff silk gazar – the supergazar that he had specially developed by Abraham's Gustav Zumstag, the Swiss fabric manufacturer, so that he could tailor his evening gowns as crisply as his suits.

However, in May 1968, Balenciaga suddenly decided he had had enough. Recognising that there was no longer a market for his fine couture, he told Prudence Glynn of the *Times*, "The life which supported couture is finished. Real couture is a luxury, which is just impossible to do anymore. Givenchy still does it because he knows, he has seen what the real

thing is like, but he has to do ready-to-wear and the boutiques too and the work is killing. No sooner has one finished one collection you must start another, no rest, no respite."[10]

There were ten workrooms at Balenciaga, four for tailoring, four for dresses and two for hats. The Social Security payments were some incredible sum – around FF 5,200 (€793/£662/$1,057) per day – and the overheads and the insurance and everything had become overwhelming. "Nobody knows what a hard métier it is. How killing is the work. Under all this luxury and glamour...it's a dog's life!"[11]

After 30 years of working in Paris, Balenciaga retired, returning to live in his beloved Spain. Balenciaga was last seen in public on 13 January 1971 at the funeral mass of Gabrielle Chanel, whom he had first met playing baccarat in the casino of San Sebastian; he had persuaded a Jesuit priest to introduce him. He came out of retirement just once, to design the dress for the marriage of General Franco's granddaughter, Dona Maria del Carmen Martinez-Bordiu y Franco, to Prince Alfonso de Borbon y Dampierre in Madrid on 9 March 1972. Balenciaga died two weeks later, on 23 March 1972. *Women's Wear Daily* headlined its story, "The King is Dead."

The *Golden Age* of the French couture was over; and women were ready for a new generation of designers who would offer innovative style, freedom of choice, and a new fashion system that provided access to all.

OPPOSITE A pared down 1960s Balenciaga navy worsted suit with white linen collar, longer jacket and knee length skirt.

ABOVE Camera-shy Cristobal Balenciaga averts his gaze away from the photographer's lens as a handsome young man in the 1920s.

3 All You Need is Love

At the close of the 1950s, the glamour and formality of haute couture had lost its glitter. Rebellion was in the air. The elitism of the early post-war years was of little interest to a new generation whose disposable income had grown through full employment. Not interested in status symbols, accents or class, this youthful group was determinedly egalitarian. Pretence was just not their scene.

No longer was it the rich, the establishment, who set the fashion, nor was the choice of clothing a sure sign of a woman's social position. The influence shifted to the inexpensive little dress seen in the High Street on girls who were ready to try anything new. This new generation and workforce demanded fashion they could identify as their own, not simply duplicates of their mothers' style.

As private fortunes dwindled and the cost of couture became impossibly high, many wholesalers responded by producing more accessible adaptations of popular couture models at moderate prices. In France the prêt-a-porter side of fashion was developing and in Italy dress manufacturing was beginning to be taken seriously and on a much larger scale.

FASHION IN THE WHITE HOUSE

In America the young and glamorous first lady, Jacqueline Kennedy, was instrumental in portraying and defining a particularly fresh and elegant style. She loved clothes and was fond of Givenchy and his pared down designs – she wore Givenchy at the funeral of her husband, President John F. Kennedy. However, when she became America's First Lady it was her close friend Oleg Cassini she chose as her personal and exclusive dress designer and Roy Halston as her milliner.

Oleg Cassini had dressed movie stars in Hollywood where he worked for Paramount Pictures as one of Edith Head's design assistants. Once married to movie actress Gene Tierney and later engaged to Grace Kelly, his new appointment established him as a top designer. He coordinated every aspect of Mrs. Kennedy's wardrobe, from shoes and hats to gloves and handbags, and although at times he may have borrowed ideas from Paris

OPPOSITE Oleg Cassini in the 1940s with his glamorous film star wife, Gene Tierney.

RIGHT Jacqueline Kennedy wore this elegant pink Alaskine silk coat by Oleg Cassini, with matching straw hat by Halston, to meet Prime Minister Nehru on her arrival in New Delhi, India, in March 1962.

couture, he served her well. Under his wing Jacqueline Kennedy became the most admired and emulated woman in the world. The many ensembles he created for her were elegant, well-made and appropriate for the occasion.

THE DEVELOPMENT OF AMERICAN SPORTSWEAR

Fashion was big business in the US. Mass production had already made fashion accessible to the wider population. American designers such as Geoffrey Beene, Anne Klein, Herbert Kasper, Bonnie Cashin and Anne Fogarty were instrumental in the development of American sportswear: a mode of dressing in luxurious separates that at the time did not exist in Europe.

Bonnie Cashin was from the West Coast and brought much of her Californian ease and experience working as a Hollywood costume designer on numerous films, ranging from modern dress for *Laura* to period costume for *Anna and the King of Siam*, into her collections. She moved to New York in 1949 and started designing clothes. Almost immediately recognised as a formidable talent, she won a Coty Award and a Neiman-Marcus Award, both in 1950.

In 1953 she opened her own design studio and realised young marrieds were moving out of the city for a safer, more fulfilling, family life. She perceived that these new women would require special fashions – clothes that would suit the country but would also be at home in the city. She started designing clothes that are now as familiar as a T-shirt – clothes for a lifestyle. "Back in the fifties," she said with sincerity in

ABOVE A 1950 two-piece bathing suit design by Bonnie Cashin, pictured with a model at a studio fashion show for buyers in New York.

OPPOSITE Known as the queen of American sportswear; a Bonnie Cashin shaggy plaid pullover with leather bound neckline and slim leather pants.

1966, "Some people didn't look as if they were in the twentieth century".[1]

She introduced ideas from all walks of life and had the ability to see relationships between objects and ideas far removed from the fashion world. From Western ranch life came the poncho, long before they became part of the Hippy uniform; fringed suede, way ahead of the trend in the late sixties. The clothes she saw worn in Chinatown became the genesis of the layered look which was developed by Cashin into a complete system of layers – a good decade before this look hit Europe.

Many professionals believed Geoffrey Beene to be not only the best American designer, but also the best fashion designer in the world. He was born in Haynesville, Louisiana. First studying medicine, he moved to New York as soon as he could to study fashion. From 1946 Beene attended the Traphagen School of Fashion. He worked at a number of fashion houses in New York and went to Paris before starting his own company back in New York.

In 1963 he began working as most couturiers do, on the form or on a live mannequin believing that was the only way to realise perfection. Known for his masterful draping, artful seaming, and fluid-yet-tailored silhouettes, his garments spoke a modern, richly sculptural language whether in form-fitting jersey or romantic clouds of brightly printed chiffon. His clothes were perfectly balanced even when he mixed unlikely fabrics together such as expensive double-faced silks with plastic trimmings. He challenged the American fashion establishment with designs that married comfort, luxury and whimsy and was appreciated by

LEFT Designed by
Geoffrey Beene in 1965,
a perfectly proportioned
drop-waist day dress
in a bold polka-dot
pattern pique with flower
decoration.

OPPOSITE Donna Karan
and Louis Dell'Olio
worked together at Anne
Klein. Donna Karan was
chosen to head up the
design team in 1974.

loyal clients including three president's wives – Lady Bird Johnson, Pat Nixon and Nancy Reagan, not to mention every fashion editor in town and several Hollywood movie stars. His career in fashion spanned over 40 years and his legacy lives on – several of his former apprentices, Kay Unger, Alber Elbaz and Doo Ri Chung, are now successful designers in their own right.

Anne Klein, like Geoffrey Beene, studied at the Traphagen School of Fashion in New York, establishing her eponymous fashion business in 1968 with her second husband, Mathew Rubinstein. She enjoyed several successful years designing highly wearable clothes for the working woman but in 1974, aged just 51, she died of breast cancer. It was then decided by new Japanese backers, Takihyo, to promote the assistant, Donna Karan, who a decade later became a household name, to head the design team.

Before launching under her own name, Anne Klein had built a reputation from a previous clothing company formed with her first

Kasper, as he was known, served in the US Army in Europe. After military service in World War II, where he designed costumes for the troupe shows in which he took part as a chorus boy, Kasper enrolled at Parsons School of Design in New York. He then spent two years in Paris perfecting his skills, with a short period at L'École de la Chambre Syndicale de la Couture Parisienne and positions at Jacques Fath, Christian Dior and Marcel Rochas.

Kasper's talent was for making inexpensive clothes look exquisite and expensive. He returned to New York and in 1963 started making clothes under his own label. For this he was rewarded with the prestigious Coty Award for American designers. But it was not until he was chosen to take over the flourishing Leslie Fay, Co Inc., when Joan Leslie died in 1966, that Kasper really flourished. He had a way of relaxing clothes without altering their function. For example, a jacket could look as soft as a cardigan, his trousers tended to be full and flowing.

Couture clothes at sportswear prices – a plain long dress might be enlivened by woven fabric with glistening threads or embroidered embellishment just around the neckline.

Kasper took what he had learned working in the Paris couture houses to the masses of America. Providing American women with affordable clothing they could mix and match to form a comprehensive and, ultimately, a contemporary wardrobe to meet every occasion.

Anne Fogarty worked as a model and advertising copywriter in New York before becoming a fashion designer in the late 1940s.

OPPOSITE A yellow sundress with striped side panels and matching button detail sun hat, by American designer, Leslie Fay.

ABOVE A group of fashion professionals – on floor, designer Anne Fogarty wearing one of her own designs, with husband, Thomas, Cathy McManus of *Vogue* and Jeane Saxer of the New York store, Lord & Taylor).

husband, Ben Klein, called Junior Sophisticates. Junior Sophisticates was a clothing label that celebrated youth, revolutionising the junior market, doing away with the traditional 'little–girl' clothing that featured button and bow detailing and addressing the desire for teenagers to look more stylish, more polished but in an individual, new way.

Herbert Kasper and Anne Fogarty are less familiar design names in Europe although they were recognised as being hugely influential in the formation of the 'American Look'.

Between 1948 and 1950 Fogarty designed clothes for the Youth Guild. Youth Guild's market, as the name suggests, was teenage girls, who were perfect for the narrow waist and full skirts of the 'New Look', a silhouette Fogarty used to perfect her much sought after dresses throughout the 50s. In 1962 she opened her own business, Anne Fogarty, Inc., where she adapted her design ideas to suit the times. Her sheath dresses often had an Empire waist. Her designs retained softness and elegance yet were youthful and innovative. She also made good use of new fabrics like Dacron that allowed soft movement (say with sunray pleating) without fullness. In the late sixties her ethnic looks led the way with pretty blouses with ruffles, and peasant skirts.

FASHION AND POPULAR CULTURE

In the democratic spirit of the times, fashion was more influenced by music, musicians and movie stars than by royalty, aristocrats and high society. The world's teenagers were regrouping, forming countercultures where rapidly changing 'street style' became their style.

Young people around the globe danced to American rock'n'roll music. In New York and San Francisco, the so-called beat generation 'dropped out' and their heroes were the writers Jack Kerouac, William Burroughs and Allen Ginsberg. They were the cool crowd who had long, intellectual conversations, denounced materialism, professed anarchy, listened to modern jazz, read poetry aloud and experimented with drugs. 'Being cool'

BELOW LEFT Known as the Beats, this cool group hung out in a New York café. Left to right: Larry Rivers, Jack Kerouac, Gregory Corso, David Amram and Allen Ginsberg.

OPPOSITE In their Mod best, from left to right, singers Cilla Black, Petula Clark and Sandy Shaw at the Dorchester Hotel for a Variety Club luncheon in 1965.

so long as it's black". They read Sartre and Camus, and congregated on the Left Bank to question not only established values and conventions, but also existence itself. Juliet Greco was the Left Bank fashion symbol whether dressed in slacks and black beret or one of her favourite Balmain dresses.

In London there were more tribes than anywhere else. 'Teddy Boys' were one of the first. In the early 50s, these young, fully-employed and mostly working-class lads took up the dandified Edwardian look that Savile Row tailors were promoting and made it their own. They wore the classic 'drainpipe' trousers with long, velvet-collared jackets and then gave the look an edge by adding crepe-soled shoes called 'brothel creepers', thin maverick ties and the ubiquitous 'DA' hairstyle. The Rockers, also called 'ton-up boys' or 'coffee-bar cowboys', hung out in small cafes drinking coffee, showing-off their motorcycles, and challenging each other to race. They wore tough, black leathers to sit astride their high-powered motorbikes. Marlon Brando in *The Wild One* was their hero.

One of the largest counterculture groups was the clean-cut Mods. They mostly chose the American Ivy League look, based on a style popular with American college students. For the girls, the look comprised A-line skirts reaching just below the knee with good quality knitwear, completed with sensible 'Hush Puppies' (granny-style lace-up shoes). Suede or leather coats and jackets were popular. Although it started as a predominantly male subculture, the Mods demonstrated a strong unisex style that would be hugely influential in years to come.

essentially meant being in the know – and not necessarily wearing clothes from an expensive fashion house. With an indifference to fashion, the American Beats wore anonymous workwear and classically comfortable clothes, typically old jeans or chinos, sloppy-joe jumpers and checked shirts.

In France their Parisian counterparts exaggerated this look. The Existentialists subscribed to Henry Ford's dictum, "Any colour

Some of the Mod boys favoured contemporary, continental styles – adaptations of Italian-style modernist tailoring, often custom-made by a local tailor, consisting of a short jacket with narrow lapels, slim trousers and button-down collared shirts with a narrow knitted tie. Italian-made sportswear was also considered cool. These outfits were worn with pointed toe shoes or desert boots and went with their favourite mode of transport – the Vespa or Lambretta scooter.

Denim jeans such as Levi's were not yet widely available in Europe, but there was a plentiful supply of a US army classic – the fishtail parka. These were personalised with an array of badges. The girls also took ideas from American rock'n'roll dance fashions. Popular styles were classic three button polo shirts worn under chunky cardigans, always over the essential pointy shaped bras; and either full skirts that were held out by layers of nylon petticoats stiffened with sugar starch, short tartan kilts or pencil skirts that flared out at the hem in an array of box pleats, worn with tight Shetland crew neck sweaters, knee-high socks and loafers. Mods would sit through 'New Wave' continental films. To be modern was to be international and this generation saw themselves as citizens of the world – albeit their own small world. It did not matter where you had come from, but where you were going.

ABOVE Mod icon, singer Julie Driscoll. Her rendition of *Wheel's on Fire* was a hit in 1968 and became the theme tune for British TV's fashion comedy *Absolutely Fabulous*.

OPPOSITE A portrait of Mary Quant and husband, Alexander Plunkett Greene, photographed at their home in London in 1965.

MARY QUANT

In 1955 London's young designers were full of ideas, but found it difficult to translate these ideas into sales. It was at this time that Mary Quant opened Bazaar, the first boutique of its kind in London at 183a King's Road, Chelsea. Born in Blackheath on the outskirts of London, she had trained in fine arts at Goldsmiths College. With her husband Alexander Plunkett Greene and friend Archie McNair providing the business backup, she jumped head first into retail.

The Bazaar venture was successful and profitable from the start. Quant's original idea was to buy and sell clothes for the young creatives and socialites who gravitated towards the King's Road. Known by the media as the 'Chelsea Set', they made Chelsea synonymous with a new way of living and dressing.

At first Quant had trouble finding the right designs and found manufacturers inflexible. However, she was not deterred and began sourcing designs from art students as well as making up her own designs, with much of her inspiration drawn from the people who passed by her shop window. She was quoted as saying at the time, "Snobbery has gone out of fashion, and in our shops you will find duchesses jostling with typists to buy the same dresses."[2]

Despite Quant's scant knowledge of dressmaking, after a few evening classes, some adaptations to commercial paper patterns, and using fabrics bought at retail prices from Harrods, she produced her first original designs. She named her short shift dress the *mini* after her favourite car; it became her trademark.[3] She celebrated youth, fun and a vague

bohemianism. Mary Quant's Bazaar was still an upmarket experience, beyond the pockets of most young Londoners; but the emphasis Quant placed on the girl, rather than the woman, was a radical development that would reshape fashion for much of the coming decade.

Within seven years Mary Quant's business was worth a million pounds, which in the early sixties was staggering. In 1963 she opened a second branch of her shop in Knightsbridge, and launched her own lower-priced label, Ginger Group, to bring her designs to the mass market. Her distinctive daisy logo appeared on many new products including make-up, tights, shoes and underwear. In 1964 she went on a tour of the US, shortly after the Beatles, and secured a ten-year licensing agreement with J.C. Penney, the first major US retailer to recognise the importance of the *mini*.

LEFT The first Mary Quant shop, called Bazaar, at 183a King's Road, Chelsea; The daisy logo prominently painted on the window.

OPPOSITE Slim trousers in black and beige wool check; matching check wool pencil skirt and jacket. Both Mary Quant Ginger Group.

Ernestine Carter, one of the most influential fashion writers of the time, wrote of Quant in her *Sunday Times* column: "It is given to a fortunate few to be born at the right time, in the right place, with the right talents. In recent fashion there are three: Chanel, Dior and Mary Quant".[4]

Some of Quant's most popular designs were her experimental mixes such as sweater dresses with plastic collars, two-tone drop-waist dresses with box pleat skirts, knickerbockers and stretch stockings in a rainbow of colours and patterns. Other typical designs were knee-length white plastic lace-up boots, often called *go-go boots*, tight ribbed sweaters in bold stripes and short shiny plastic raincoats, zipped at the front. These clothes all became part of the 'London Look'.

Britain's art schools were flourishing and by the late 50s many had set up pioneering fashion

and textile departments and were producing a host of talented young graduates who, encouraged by Mary Quant's success, set up their own workrooms. The Royal College of Art (RCA) had the largest and most sought after fashion department, and was soon recognised as the breeding ground for some of the most exciting and innovative fashion talent in the country.

THE RCA AND THE RISE OF THE BOUTIQUES

In the fifties and sixties the RCA was at the centre of the explosion of Pop Art culture, a vibrant, invigorating movement that waved goodbye to Britain's post-war austerity. At its head, the eminent Professor Janey Ironside, a former fashion journalist, nurtured the talents of many iconic names in fashion: Marion Foale and Sally Tuffin, Ossie Clark, Bill Gibb and Zandra Rhodes, to name a few.

In response to the demand for more affordable, fast-moving and youthful fashions, boutiques were springing up all over central London; many of the best were started by Royal College of Art graduates. James Wedge, Marion Foale and Sally Tuffin all made names for themselves in the sixties. Wedge, originally a highly successful milliner working for couturier Ronald Paterson, was joint owner with Pat Booth of über-trendy King's Road boutiques Top Gear and Countdown, which offered a total look, importing hip and exclusive French labels. Top Gear was a tiny shop with light bulbs all the way around with a little dressing room and blacked out windows. Wedge said, "It was all black inside with scaffolding for the coat

OPPOSITE Advertisement for Mary Quant cosmetics featuring a naked model embellished with the familiar daisy motif that appeared on the Quant make-up packaging.

ABOVE A beret and scarf in yellow and red dyed rabbit fur by the milliner turned fashion entrepreneur James Wedge, who later became a fashion photographer.

hangers and a mirror that fitted the end wall. We had a carrier bag with a bull's eye printed on it, no name or anything, just a bull's eye. People knew where that carrier bag came from. Tiny and dark but the customers were as trendy as they came: rock and rollers, the Beatles and on Saturdays there was always a Rolling Stone. Marianne Faithful used to be in there on a regular basis. All the 'beautiful people' used to hang out there".[5]

With their bright, amusing designs, Foale & Tuffin, who established their business in 1961, became essential suppliers to James Wedge's boutiques and other fashionable shops such as Wollands, Liberty and the newly opened Browns in South Molton Street. In the early days, Zandra Rhodes designed fabric for the duo. Their increasing popularity prompted the pair to open their own showroom, just off Carnaby Street, which they eventually converted into a retail outlet.

Foale & Tuffin became every fashionable girl's first destination for individual and well-made clothes. Marion said, "We were fed on couture, which we absolutely loved at the time, we were taught to cut and sew properly from the start – bound buttonholes, pockets with welts, work on a stand."[6] Sally: "We visited couture houses, we went to Paris – Chanel, Dior, Givenchy and Balenciaga."[7] Inspiration and skills acquired from these observations and a classical education in high fashion at the RCA were eloquently translated into delightful clothes, relished by the youth market, that they could enjoy and afford.

Foale & Tuffin's first shift dresses were printed with American art images, pop art and mod targets, triangles and zig zags in primary colours. They also experimented successfully with mixing and matching patterns in one garment. They mixed tartan patterns, pieced together small floral Liberty prints in different colourways, and combined different colours of spotted cotton seersucker together on trousers, smocks and tiered pinafore dresses. Along with John Bates, who designed the sleek, ready-for-action clothes Diana Rigg wore as Emma Peel in the cult TV show *The Avengers*, they were the first designers in London to show really short skirts, which had been creeping up the leg since 1959.

Foale & Tuffin also popularised trouser suits, possibly before Yves Saint Laurent's Le *Smoking* created a global sensation in 1966. In 1965 they made a corduroy jacket for model Jill Kennington and decided to put it together with matching trousers. Sally Tuffin said, "We thought it hilarious and it was pretty daring at the time, but she looked wonderful in them. It was so comfortable wearing trousers and, remarkably, there weren't many trousers for women you could buy at the time. And there was always this problem with mini-skirts and what you put on your legs. Stockings were flesh coloured, fine denier and worn with suspender belts. We wanted fun colours, and thicker as well. We found these wonderful Swedish stockings, which we sold in our shop. And I think the trouser suit revolution was just a feeling in the air that had to happen."[8]

THE CHANGING MOOD IN PARIS

The mood was changing in Paris as well. While the dictates of the couture seemed irrelevant to a young and fast growing market, there were many new ready-to-wear designers, known as stylists, successfully spreading their wings in Paris. These included Dorothée Bis, who designed exciting new knitted garments; Emmanuelle Khanh, whose gentle, feminine shapes and curvy tailoring were copied everywhere; and Sonia Rykiel, with distinctive knitwear and feminine style. The Victoire boutique on the Place Victoire became an important Parisian showcase for promoting new French design talent.

Nevertheless, it was London, the beat of pop music and the teenage culture that was taking a firm grip of the fashion world. And when the shift dress appeared in Paris in 1957, Paris finally took Mary Quant's London look seriously, for the new shape had been seen at Bazaar at least 18 months before. These simple shapes were perfect for the new synthetic materials such as Tricel, Trevira and Dacron which were used enthusiastically by designers to create these cutting-edge and somewhat futuristic looks.

In France, Yves Saint Laurent's attempt at rebellion with his 1960 all-black, *Beat* collection for Dior was a flop with Dior's establishment clientele. As a result, the management at Dior replaced Saint Laurent with Marc Bohan, releasing Yves Saint Laurent for military service. Suffering a nervous breakdown after only a few weeks, Saint Laurent was hospitalised and then released from the army in November. He sued Dior for breach of contract, and won.

ABOVE Geometric blocks of colour shift dress with cut-out side panels, designed by French designer Emmanuelle Khanh for I.D. and worn by sixties model Peggy Moffat.

OPPOSITE From Yves Saint Laurent's *Beat* collection for Dior, model Enid Boulting wears a black leather jacket, helmet and high crocodile boots.

By 1962 the French intelligentsia had been refreshed by philosophers Michel Foucault and Roland Barthes, and anthropologist Claude Levi-Strauss; along with the *nouvelle vague* film directors, Jean-Luc Goddard and Francoise Truffaut. The time was right for something new on the Paris fashion scene, and Saint Laurent established his own fashion house with the help of his business partner Pierre Bergé.

THE NEW SPIRIT OF THE MID-60S

During the 1960s a new style of photography was developed by a group of young, predominantly working-class British fashion photographers who were determined to make names for themselves. The models were shot realistically on location and in highly exaggerated, animated poses contrasting sharply with the haughty upper class looks that had become the norm. David Bailey, Terence Donovan, Brian Duffy, John French and Norman Parkinson used hand-held cameras, often with telephoto lenses. Other trend-setting photographers were Helmut Newton, Barry Lattigan, Guy Boudin and Peter Knapp. They dominated the glossy pages of *Vogue*, *Queen*, *Elle* and *Harper's Bazaar*.

Their models, such as Jean Shrimpton, Twiggy, Jill Kennington, Veruschka, Celia Hammond, Tania Mallet and Sandra Paul, soon became household names. These photographers and models were so influential that the legendary Italian film director Michelangelo Antonioni made the iconic film *Blow Up* (1966), loosely based on the life of 'Swinging' London's egotistic photographic scene.

ABOVE *Queen* magazine was the handbook for the hip and fashionable in the swinging sixties and Veruschka the supermodel of her day. Dress by Princess Luciana.

OPPOSITE A group of sixties models wear a variety of trouser styles including ski pants, a wide leg style, velvet classics and a design in a jazzy plaid pattern.

of gallery goers in the 1960s *Whaam!* stood as the ultimate image of the new in art.

The music scene exploded with the sensational sound of The Beatles' *Love Me Do* in Britain and Bob Dylan's first album, simply entitled *Bob Dylan,* in the States. The sixties was also an era of sexual freedom. The contraceptive pill was invented and the women's liberation movement activated; in Britain abortion was legalised in 1967. The new freedom was reflected in the era's fashion trends.

THE START OF THE SWINGING SIXTIES

Time Magazine's exemplary cover illustration of the "Swinging Sixties" in 1966 extolling the love affair with liberated youth, the mini-skirted, Beatles-and-Biba-mad, flower-powered sixties when every fashion tenet was broken, when London was 'in' and practically everything that had gone before was 'out', really started to swing around 1964. That was the year Karl Lagerfeld left Jean Patou to freelance, Zandra Rhodes graduated from the RCA, Sonia Rykiel began designing innovative knitwear for her husband's Paris boutique, *Laura,* and Rudi Gernreich, a former dancer, introduced the no-bra bra to underline the spare, body-hugging fashions he designed in flexible silk jersey. Ossie Clark began designing for Woollands prior to graduating in 1965 and Bridget Riley's Op Art designs dominated the art market. Every new film seemed to set another trend: *Jules et Jim, Bonnie & Clyde, Doctor Zhivago.* Jean Muir's star was also rising. In 1964 she won the first of her three Dress of The Year awards, given by the Bath Fashion Museum, for a Jane & Jane dress in printed Liberty silk.

LEFT Jean Shrimpton in 1964 wearing a black and white polka-dot, short fitted dress in crepe by Mary Quant with ruffle cuffs and collar.

ABOVE Jean Muir wears a dress of her own design in white wool bouclé in the shape she made famous, from her first independent collection of 1967.

In 1962 pop artists Andy Warhol, Roy Lichtenstein and Claes Oldenburg were the New Realists and a smash hit on the Manhattan art season. A few months later a group of British pop artists including David Hockney, Allen Jones and Peter Blake took the Paris Biennale by storm and when the Tate Gallery bought Roy Lichtenstein's painting *Whaam!* in 1966 it "aroused more public interest than almost any purchase since the war."[9] And for a generation

BIBA

Barbara Hulanicki's Biba brand became one of the biggest success stories of the decade. Hulanicki worked as a fashion illustrator after studying at Brighton Art College in the late 1950s. She married advertising executive Stephen Fitz-Simon and they soon opened a mail order clothing company that she named Biba's Postal Boutique, Biba being the nickname of her young sister Biruta.

In May 1964 Hulanicki was commissioned by Felicity Greene, fashion editor of the *Daily Mirror*, to design a dress for her pages. It was a sleeveless pink gingham shift dress with a hole cut out at the back of the neck with a matching triangular kerchief à la Brigitte Bardot, offered to the readers for the very modest sum of 25 shillings (about £1.25/$2/€1.45) in today's money). As you can imagine, for that price the business was overwhelmed with orders – in fact, more than seventeen thousand.

This little Biba dress was, in a way, reaping the harvest from the seeds Mary Quant had sown. Bazaar had promised youth and fun, but it was still catering for the elite. Barbara Hulanicki, on the other hand, was offering sophistication that almost everyone could afford, and the response was overwhelming. Barbara had insisted, "I didn't want to make clothes for kept women, I wanted to make clothes for people in the street, and Fitz and I always tried to get prices down, down to the bare minimum."[10]

The first Biba boutique opened in September of 1964 at 87 Abingdon Road, West London, and word spread quickly through fashion magazines and newspapers and via the popular music shows on television. There was no sign outside the first boutique; the windows were blacked out, the walls painted navy blue and the floor graphic black and white. The clothes were displayed on Victorian bentwood coat stands instead of standard rails because they were cheap and cheerful.

The shop played songs by The Beatles repeatedly; it was the only album they had. The louder the music, the longer the queue became; sometimes right around the block. The boutique was also the first shop to stay open until 8 p.m.

Another stroke of luck for Biba came from Cathy McGowan, whose TV show, *Ready, Steady, Go*, was one of the most popular music shows of the moment. Known as Queen of Mods, she loved the Biba clothes she had seen featured in *Honey* magazine, the consumer bible for young girls in the sixties. Hulanicki was delighted when McGowan asked to wear her clothes to present her TV show. She could not have wished for a better advertisement than McGowan, who she admired and said "possessed such youthful sophistication".

Biba girls copied Cathy McGowan's long, straight hair and eye-covering fringe,

OPPOSITE Pauline Stone in the gingham check Barbara Hulanicki dress for Biba inspired by Brigit Bardot that sold more than 17,000 by mail order, published in the *Daily Mirror* in 1964.

LEFT Queen of the Mods, Cathy McGowan, star of the television music programme *Ready Steady Go*, relaxing offset in 1965 in a Foale & Tuffin starburst shift dress.

their eyelids weighed down with doll-like fake eyelashes. With their slender bodies and matchstick legs encased in pale tights and low-cut pumps, they seldom needed elasticated corsets (known then as roll-ons) or bras, which further promoted a wonderful feeling of total liberation from past sartorial conventions. Biba's customers had to be slender because the long, skinny sleeves were so tight they almost stopped your circulation.

Biba's second best seller was little more than an extended, classic striped rugby shirt dyed in sludgy colours, which sold for about 3 guineas in old money or £3.15 ($5.04/€3.65) in today's currency. Another popular seller was a T-shirt adapted from an old-fashioned plain cotton vest or undershirt with a ribbon running through the neckline, available in about 20 different colours. Sales of these items numbered six figures.

OPPOSITE A best-selling short, skinny vest dress by Biba in bold black, red and white striped cotton jersey.

RIGHT Biba's purple knee-high canvas boots also came in dusty shades in soft suede. The perfect accessory for both long and short skirts, hot pants and jumpsuits.

Biba soon graduated to larger premises, first to Kensington Church Street, then Kensington High Street where they introduced menswear and more accessories including the hugely successful knee-length canvas boots that came in delicious dusty pastel shades. Every visiting celebrity seemed to go to Biba; including Princess Anne who often came in with her lady-in-waiting. Their biggest thrill, however, was when Brigitte Bardot came in with her new husband, the German playboy, Gunther Sachs.

Young girls would flock to the boutique on Saturdays to soak up the dark, mysterious atmosphere and lose themselves in the loud music – whether it was Billie Holiday, the Beatles, the Rolling Stones or the Kinks. It was not unusual for 30,000 people to pass through the door on Saturdays. This was a new shopping experience for the young office workers who could blow their minds as well as their week's wages on Biba's glamorous offerings and walk out feeling like celebrities in long, flowing dresses, feather boas, striped knitwear, hats, patterned tights and knee-high canvas boots. Shoplifting was rife, as the crowded communal changing room and laid-back attitude of the sales girls made it easy for the light-fingered to get away with swapping old clothes for new, and then walking out without paying.

CARNABY STREET

Narcissistic dressing up was a male as well as a female option and for a dedicated follower of fashion, Carnaby Street became a conduit – not only for fashion, but also for rapid social and material change. Men had certainly become more interested in clothes and since the 1967

RIGHT Quintessentially Biba. Twiggy in a glamorous 1930s style evening dress and coat in pale gold satin, stretched out luxuriously on a leopard skin bed.

reform to decriminalise sexual acts between consenting males over 21, along with the influence of pop musicians, they were less afraid of being suspected of homosexuality. Dressing up was fun whether it was in a ruffled shirt, a bright red military band jacket, loon trousers or a psychedelic print tie – or indeed, all three worn at once.

The fashion industry saw a potential new market and men's clothing became brighter and more adventurous. Pre-1960s Carnaby Street was just an ordinary urban thoroughfare housing low end workshops above regular High Street bakers, hairdressers and ironmongers' stores. The only nearby clothing store was Vince, offering outré styles to a clientele of chorus boys and sports celebrities associated with the West End's still criminalised gay scene.

Menswear entrepreneur John Stephen was one of the first to open in the street but soon

LEFT London's Carnaby Street in 1967 where the Lord John boutique could not be missed and where the Ravel shoe shop was thriving.

an endless stream of 'boutiques' followed
– The Man's Shop, Adam, His Clothes, Male
West One and more offering all the latest
gear, squarely targeted at the male consumer.
Carnaby Street soon became a magnet for
tourists with its Union Jack festooned facades.
Now pedestrianised and full of souvenir
emporia, its glory days are over; however,
while it lasted the street perfectly captured and
coloured our understanding of the period.

PARIS RECAPTURES ITS YOUTH

In Paris, the leading designers lost no time in
joining the youth movement. André Courrèges
rocketed to fame in 1964 when he introduced
his seminal collection in Paris. His clean-lined,
space-age inspired designs included 'astronaut'
hats and goggles, white and silver 'moon girl'
loon trousers, cat suits and white patent or
kid leather mid-calf length boots that became
the ultimate status symbol worn with skirts at

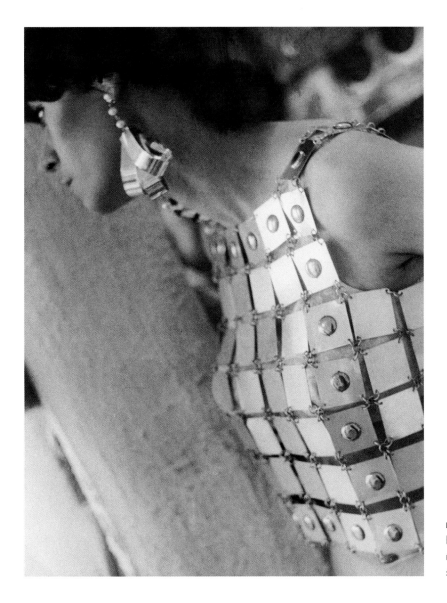

LEFT A detail of a Paco
Rabanne chain mail dress
made up from linked
silver plastic squares.

LEFT A short pastel pink wool gabardine coat by Courrèges photographed to coincide with the opening of the Courrèges room at Harrods.

OPPOSITE A wave stripe evening dress in multi-coloured sequins and tuxedo suit, both designed by Pierre Cardin, appeared in a 1965 issue of *Queen* magazine.

a shockingly short, above-the-knee length. In London Quant's skirts were short but what Courrèges offered now were most definitely shorter. Quant immediately raised hers to thigh length and so it went on – or up.

Paco Rabanne was the son of a former head seamstress at Balenciaga, real name Francisco Rabaneda Cuervo. Noted for his unconventional use of materials, he took the sixties look to its extreme. Inspired by America's and Russia's space programmes, his first 'body jewellery' collection of 1966 consisted of shift dresses constructed from plastic or metal discs and tiles, linked with wire or chain. Personified by his costumes for Jane Fonda in *Barbarella*, Rabanne saw women as the new Amazons; they were liberated, dominating, and therefore fated for the life of a warrior. "My chain mail clothes stood witness to that," Paco Rabanne was noted as saying.[11]

Italian-born Pierre Cardin also loved geometric shapes; his avant-garde designs were the bubble-dress and colour blocked sheaths, often covered with his signature bull's eye prints and cut-outs, and the collarless, Beatles jacket. Cardin was the first couturier to launch a ready-to-wear collection, at Paris department store Printemps in 1959; as well as the first to open Japan as a high fashion market in the same year. He amassed a great fortune through his business arrangements such as his highly successful uniform designs for Pakistan International Airlines, and his Espace Cardin (a theatre) launched in 1971. His business acumen has been a fine example to many designers since and he is one of the few of his generation still active in fashion today.

ABOVE Thumbnail sketches of the key looks for 1965 from Parisian designer Emanuel Ungaro, with hairstyles by Vidal Sassoon.

OPPOSITE Yves Saint Laurent's three-piece *Le Smoking* trouser suit was an instant hit back in 1967 and remains a timeless classic to this day.

Emanuel Ungaro, who had worked with Courrèges at Balenciaga for six years before starting up on his own in 1965, followed suit, sculpting hard-edged clothes in heavy worsted fabrics and triple gabardines to retain an angular shape, almost standing up by themselves.

In 1966 Yves Saint Laurent opened his ready-to-wear Rive Gauche boutique, which quickly expanded to 160 branches worldwide. He received financial backing, arranged by his partner and astute business associate Pierre Bergé, from a variety of sources including the cosmetics company, Charles of the Ritz.

OPPOSITE The iconic
Mondrian inspired shift
dress by Yves Saint
Laurent. This version
made in white double
jersey with black cross
and red square.

His debut collection had depicted the gamine style popularised by the film *Jules et Jim*, but it was not until he launched the much copied, colour-blocked Mondrian collection in 1965, and again in 1966, when he presented his famous *Le Smoking* trouser suit for women that he became a major player on the international fashion stage. Pierre Bergé said that Coco Chanel had given women freedom, adding that YSL gave them power, reducing the sartorial differences between men and women.

Grace Mirabella of American *Vogue* had also declared on the pages of *In and Out of Vogue*, that the YSL pantsuit marked the beginning of a new concept of what constituted sophisticated day dressing, which had a profound influence on the later work of such designers as Calvin Klein and Giorgio Armani. Yves Saint Laurent's love of the exotic also led him to be the first couturier to use black and Asian models.

THE FASHION EDITORS

Saint Laurent was the darling of a new generation of journalists. These were adventurous individuals looking for the best new talent to personify their life and times after decades of predictably tasteful but now tired fashion. The young heir to *Women's Wear Daily*, John Fairchild, became editor-in-chief following a spell living and working in Paris, and appreciated YSL's fresh approach to couture. Diana Vreeland had been poached from *Harper's Bazaar* and was now the exciting new editor of American *Vogue*.

In Britain, under the editorship of Beatrix Miller, *Vogue* endorsed the talents of a new generation of British designers. France was fortunate to have the stylists Maïmé Arnodin and Denise Fayolle who joined forces in 1968 to set up the design consultancy Mafia that ensured the growing numbers of French prêt-a-porter designers were known on an international scale.

THE ITALIAN DESIGNERS

The up-market ready-to-wear and couture trades in Paris, Rome and New York were still in demand by the elite throughout the sixties and Italy's designers were offering colour and fine craftsmanship that were much sought after.

Italy had the formidable and much copied talent of the Marchese Emilio Pucci, who did not enter the fashion business until he was in his 40s. He worked out of Florence and was internationally known by the jet-set who could not get enough of his acid-bright, psychedelic prints made into tightly fitting silk jersey shifts, shirts, cat suits, evening dress, Capri pants and swimwear. Pucci saw his swirly designs as the forerunners of sixties Pop Art. Pucci made good use of the newly available stretch fabrics for his designs, making them perfectly glamorous for travelling by high-speed boat, convertible car or plane. "Women must move with elegance and freedom that entails a streamlined quality which is part of contemporary living," Pucci decreed.[12]

The beautiful, art-quality knitwear of Tai and Rosita Missoni, with their stripes, geometrics and abstract florals, created a sensation at the 1967 Pitti Palace showing in Florence. Missoni continues to thrive as a family business successfully retaining its original artisan values. Originating in Florence, the world-famous Gucci and Ferragamo brands began by making the best hand-crafted shoes and leather goods, which became must-haves for the international jet-set. There was a phrase created to describe this elite group of Italian couturiers – 'the Gucci-Pucci syndrome' which was indicative of *la dolce vita*, a luxurious way of life.

On the other hand there was Fiorucci, the cheeky fashion label created by Elio Fiorucci in 1967. The shop first brought London's Carnaby Street and New York's fashion trends to Milan, then expanded internationally in the 70s, using underground styles, bright colours and animal prints to create a singular look, along with introducing stretch denim and the concept of designer jeans to the market. The stores expanded to include vintage fashions as well as books, furniture, and music reflecting pop culture of the day, lasting well into the 1980s.

THE NEXT SENSATION

Throughout the decade the hemline continued to rise until you could barely call it a skirt – more than six inches above the knee at its most extreme. More practical, brightly coloured tights replaced stockings and suspenders, and underwear became minimal. Along with Vidal Sassoon's five-point haircut, the 60s look was best suited to stick-thin teenagers – epitomised by the schoolgirl model Lesley Hornby, known as Twiggy.

It was at Dior that the next sensation started when Marc Bohan introduced his maxi-length coats in 1966. *Women's Wear Daily* headlined their feature 'AGENT PROVOCATEUR', which had a full day's scoop on Marc Bohan's collection for Dior. They wrote "Stalking down Dior's ramps, models swaggered in mid-calf length capes and military greatcoats that could have stepped right out of *Doctor Zhivago*."[13]

Marc Bohan's challenge to the high-rise skirts was obvious. "Something had to be done about the length," said Bohan. "They couldn't get any shorter – and besides it's fun."[14] But his timing was off. Nobody wanted the drastic change and hemlines remained firmly well above the knee. Many women, not only teenagers, were just feeling comfortable in the mini. What really took off at this point were trousers. Tailored, casual, harem, jodhpurs, and blue jeans – anything with two legs became acceptable, while maxi coats were worn happily with ultra short skirts underneath!

REVISITING ART DECO AND ART NOUVEAU STYLE

A major exhibition held in Paris at the Musée des Arts Décoratifs in 1966 entitled *Les Années 25: Art Déco/Bauhaus/Stijl Esprit Nouveau* was one of the first signs of a revival of Art Deco and Art Nouveau in fashion. Three years later both Art Nouveau and Art Deco were given a phenomenal boost by the publication of Martin Battersby's *The Decorative Twenties*, followed in 1971 by *The Decorative Thirties*, as well as Bevis Hillier's *Art Deco of the 20s and 30s*, and fashionable people snapped up copies of these books.

Two movies endorsed the look further, with Faye Dunaway in *Bonnie & Clyde* (1967) and Mia Farrow in *The Great Gatsby* (1974) capturing a new, nostalgic love affair with the retro Deco look. In 1968 Biba produced their first catalogue designed in Art Deco style, taking

advertisements in popular magazines *Honey*, *19* and *Petticoat* that paid off handsomely with over a hundred thousand requests for a copy.

HIPPY CHIC
By 1969 fashionable eyes had turned to the West Coast of America. The film *Easy Rider* examined an American counterculture, and at the end of the decade the world saw student uprisings and protests against the war in Vietnam. The Free Music Festival at Woodstock became a symbol for the hippy movement, a movement away from futurism and modernism towards the past and the cultures of the East. The hippies and flower children, fascinated by Asian mysticism, adopted the loose tops and tunics of the East as their uniform and came to embody the search for an alternative society. They were encouraged to turn on, tune in, and drop out by LSD expert, Dr. Timothy Leary of Harvard University. Many took his advice, experimenting with drugs, abandoning social conventions and forming communal living arrangements.

That same year, in response to the insatiable appetite of the young for blue jeans, a San Francisco real estate developer named Don Fisher and his wife Doris, who were already in their forties, launched a retail format called The Gap selling only Levi's jeans. Later they would create their own brand of clothing and become global leaders in casual fashion for all the family.

LEFT Robert Redford and Mia Farrow in a scene from the original *The Great Gatsby*. Mia Farrow in typical 20s beaded frock that set a new trend in the 70s.

Meanwhile, French designers such as Jean Bouquin embraced hippy chic, transforming the look into expensive designer wear worn by Brigitte Bardot and other St. Tropez types; and Talitha Getty's Moroccan *boho* style inspired Yves Saint Laurent. Striped djellabas, harem trousers, caftans, tent shapes, rajah coats and Nehru jackets were recreated in fine wools, silks and chiffons. In Britain, Ossie Clark and Celia Birtwell, Jean Muir, Zandra Rhodes, Gina Fratina, Bill Gibb and John Bates were at the forefront of high fashion, all showing an enthusiastic interest in ethnic garments.

Biba and the London look of the 1960s had been a massive success but by the early 1970s the fashion tide had turned. In 1973, with the backing of Dorothy Perkins and British Land, Biba moved into the massive Art Deco store Derry & Toms on Kensington High Street. After restoring the building to its former glory, including a roof garden with pink flamingos and the rainbow room restaurant, Biba became a theatre for fashion. It was the ultimate fantasy department store shopping destination and Hulanicki bravely stocked its floors with everything a fashionista could dream of. It became the number one tourist attraction in London in the early seventies but the dream came to a sad and abrupt end in 1975 when Dorothy Perkins was taken over by British Land who then pulled out as investors and forced Biba into closure.

ABOVE Woodstock poster designed by Arnold Skolnick after the venue was changed at the last minute. Peace, love and good music.

OPPOSITE Twiggy sits all alone in the vast Art Deco Rainbow Room restaurant of the Biba superstore in Kensington High Street just before it closed.

4 You Are What You Wear

In the face of social upheaval, fashion in the seventies did not seem a major priority, yet the pace of change accelerated. Ideas came from far-flung places, inventions and manufacturing techniques emerged and were assimilated. Couture fashion continued producing 'classics.' And retro-chic became mainstream. The individual was celebrated, and self-expression was paramount. The writer Tom Wolf called it the "Me Decade". But which "me" to choose? That was the big question. Fashions were romantic, individualistic and unstructured. Designers were creating extravagant interpretations of Russian, Chinese, African, Indian and gypsy themes, as well as making nostalgic forays back to styles of the 20s, 30s and 40s.

The seventies provided a dressing-up box of fashion from which to choose; from old war uniforms worn for their decorative details, to Native American looks – fringed leather and suede garments with lots of colourful beads. Exotic clothes and all manner of original treasures found in thrift shops and street markets, including menswear, were plundered and refigured for the feminine shape.

With a worldwide recession, inflation, strikes, oil shortages, terrorism and political scandal, it was not surprising that escapism and a nostalgia for happier times was also reflected in fashion, which became freer than ever before.

Fashion magazines declared, "anything goes": there really were no rules.

THE NEW FACES OF FASHION PHOTOGRAPHY

Fashion photography explored many different moods, from Sarah Moon's dreamy, romantic images to the aggressive and decadent photography of Helmut Newton. The positively confident, almost aggressive poses of the 1960s depicted a fearless youth, ready for anything. However, the seventies woman was looking for more from a fashion magazine. They wanted more fantasy, more escapism – whether it was an exotic location, dramatic make-up or an alternative lifestyle down on a farm.

Magazines such as *Nova*, launched in 1965, had set a new pace to magazine publishing, combining daring and artistic imagery with unconstrained writing. The artist Molly Parkin was its first fashion director and Caroline Baker her assistant. They worked freely

OPPOSITE Model, Apollonia van Ravenstein wears a classic 1975 Missoni ensemble of stripes and chevron design in marvellously uplifting colour combinations.

RIGHT Artist Molly Parkin, the original fashion editor of *NOVA* magazine photographed in 2009 at the launch party of a collaboration between Barbara Hulanicki (Biba) and Topshop.

with the leading photographers and artists of
the day producing bold and often controversial
images of the latest trends. For its brief life of 11
years, *Nova* was a star that flared brightly and
quite suddenly faded, very much a product and
a clear mirror of its turbulent times.

Cosmopolitan magazine was another
ground-breaking publication of this time.
Following the immense success of its American
edition formulated by Helen Gurley Brown
(already famous for her book *Sex and the
Single Girl*, 1962), it was launched in the UK
in 1972 and aimed at teenage girls. *Cosmo*
was the first magazine of its kind to openly
talk about and celebrate sex. That same year
Rosie Boycott and Marsha Rowe launched
their feminist magazine, *Spare Rib,* in the UK,
and in America *Ms Magazine* was launched
by Gloria Steinem and founding editor, Letty
Cottin Pogrebin.

THE BUSINESS OF READY-TO-WEAR

Ready-to-wear fashion was on a roll, resulting
in continuing growth and prosperity for fashion
manufacturers, notably the American and
Italian ready-to-wear mass producers, and
marked the beginning of fashion as truly big
business depending heavily on marketing,
promotion, and advertising. The advancement
in manufacturing technology and expertise led
to rapid turnover in design and product. Another
aspect of fashion affected by mass production
was that department stores were entering a new
era. New York led the field and the rest of the
world followed. Saks Fifth Avenue and Bergdorf
Goodman closed down their by-now obsolete
couture and custom departments, and all stores
phased out their huge millinery salons. Instead
they divided their floors into designer boutique
areas, shuffling them around as one designer
became hotter than another. Bloomingdales

LEFT Henri Bendel
promoted the idea of the
'destination' fashion
store and nurtured new
design talent.

OPPOSITE A voluminous
tiered dress, cape and
Peruvian felt hat by
Kenzo. Illustration from a
private collection by Nino
Caprioglio.

was transformed into a place to see and be seen – one of the first 'destination' stores. Henri Bendel and, later, Barneys became the stores capable of discovering and nurturing new talents such as Stephen Burrows, John Kloss, Joan Vass and Mary McFadden. Sadly though, some of New York's formerly great stores, such as Hattie Carnegie and Jay Thorpe, vanished.

Mass production began to threaten France's leadership of the fashion world; they had brilliant creators and artisans but were never good at manufacturing for the masses. The Paris couture needed new strategies to guarantee its commercial viability in the face of mass-produced designer goods if it was to maintain the primacy that it had enjoyed for more than a century. A wave of international designers brought new life to the Paris fashion scene.

In 1970, Kenzo Takada's Jungle Jap boutique opened, decorated in wild jungle

patterns in the style of Henri Rousseau. His clothes were an immediate success with young fashion individualists such as the models who were now arriving from all over the world to work in Paris. His first collection was made entirely of cotton, much of it quilted. It was shown on photographic rather than runway models to the sound of rock music, the beginning of a trend that continues to this day.

Kenzo took folkloric ideas and translated them into fresh young, modern designs. His take on the Inca peasant, for example, went bolder and brighter; clashes of paint box primary colours and exotic floral prints inspired by his native Japan worked wonders to lift fashion from its doldrums. He revitalised his collections each season with new ideas from around the world.

Kenzo was a tireless innovator and stylist whose twice-yearly collections became the hottest ticket in Paris. Even savvy industry professionals were known to fake a 'faint' in order to get whisked in to his 'big top' shows ahead of the crush. Entrepreneur Joseph Ettedgui, who later opened a chain of eponymous shops, had the good business sense to immediately open Kenzo boutiques in London. Kenzo was also a big hit in America.

After studying at the school of the *Chambre Syndicale de la Couture Parisienne*, Issey Miyake launched his own collection in Paris in 1973. His confident, billowing shapes challenged Western traditions of tailoring, concentrating on wrapping and layering, swathing the body in loose, unstructured garments. His unusually textured and layered fabrics were a reflection of Japanese classical dress, adapted for western living. While they were marvelously dramatic in photographs, they were not yet generally understood or accepted by the mainstream.

Emmanuelle Khanh, the former Balenciaga and Givenchy model turned designer who was credited with kick starting the young ready-to-wear fashion movement in France in 1963, established her own business in 1970 and a ready-to-wear label in 1972. Khanh's designs were popular for their neat and precise styling, using soft, feminine jersey fabrics. Some of Khanh's designs were ethnic-inspired, and she also developed a line of knitwear. She ultimately became known for her designs of the biggest, most fashionable eyewear frames in a wide variety of colours and materials.

Jean-Charles de Castelbajac was also very much part of the 70s French fashion scene. His idiosyncratic designs mixed bright colours, pop culture and humour in flamboyant style. He dressed Farah Fawcett for the hit series *Charlie's Angels*. He worked with the pop artists Robert Combas and Jean-Charles Blais to create a line of pop art dresses featuring their works of art and created his famous duvet ski jacket with transparent plastic pockets filled with brightly coloured feathers, years before the ubiquitous puffa jacket appeared as a popular sports coat.

Yves Saint Laurent was in his prime and could do no wrong throughout the seventies.

RIGHT Charlotte Rampling wears a highly fashionable fringed roll-neck poncho by Emmanuelle Khanh. The boots are by Halston.

RIGHT Modelled by
Naomi Campbell for
the Yves Saint Laurent
Retrospective show in
Paris in 2002; fur coat
and shoes originally from
the controversial 1971
collection inspired by
friend, Paloma Picasso.

The influence of the YSL trouser suit had already become an essential part of a chic woman's wardrobe. He continued to shock with collections like that of autumn/winter 1971, which was thought to be inspired by 1940s ladies of the night. It was actually his friend Paloma Picasso who gave him the idea. He said, "I saw her one day coming to an event in a turban, platform shoes, one of her mother's 1940s dresses, and outrageously made up. That day she made an extreme impression on me."[1]

With broad-shouldered, primary-coloured furs worn brazenly over floral print shorts and dresses, turbans on the models' heads and platform-soled shoes on their feet, the collection was instantly dismissed as being in bad taste by the bourgeoisie, but recognised later as the way ahead.

In 1976 he created a fabulous collection of head-to-toe ethnic looks using a mix of Liberty prints for his *Rive Gauche* collection; and in the same year designed the *Carmen* collection for the haute couture. Then he delighted his followers with the marvelous *Ballets Russes* collection in April 1977 (possibly inspired by the famous Sotheby's sale of the Diaghilev ballet costumes in 1970).

By this time the mini was definitely out, looking well past its prime. The long skirt was in. *Vogue* now declared "The long skirt is here" – the first copy of *Vogue* for many years appeared with not a short skirt in sight, and more leg than ever. Hemlines went from mini to midi to maxi.

ABOVE Paloma Picasso in Paris in the seventies wearing some of her mother's vintage 1940s clothes.

OPPOSITE American model Beverly Johnson wearing a textured knit cardigan by Bonnie Cashin in 1975.

Biba did 30's Hollywood glamour big time in the shiny new Biba store from 1973 until its sad demise in 1975. Ever optimistic, Mary Quant and Tommy Roberts of Mr. Freedom went for the shortest, brightest hot pants and bright, cheery knits. Mary Quant MBE was now established as a national treasure; her achievements marked by a retrospective exhibition at the London Museum in 1973. Bill Gibb, Dorothée Bis, Perry Ellis, Bonnie Cashin, Sonia Rykiel and Missoni took their knitwear designs to the height of chic and technical finesse.

Jean Muir, known as the sculptress of fluid fabrics, crafted flattering matte jersey dresses. Her butter-soft suede and leather garments in her signature shade of navy blue, and later her colourful cashmeres, were presented elegantly twice each year from her Mayfair showroom, which had become an essential stop for international buyers. Her discreet style was appreciated by a growing number of influential working women around the world.

A SEA OF DENIM

However, by the end of the decade it was trousers that dominated – from hot pants, stovepipes and bell-bottoms to Yves Saint Laurent's perfectly feminine straight-leg classics. But it was denim that became the undisputed star of the decade. Denim had been well established in the youth market in the US and by the end of the 1960s elevated Levi-Strauss' blue jean sales to more than one hundred million pairs a year.

By 1975 denim jeans were worn everywhere with everything – from diamond encrusted T-shirts to cowboy boots. Blue jeans were the sexy alternative and the ultimate social leveler, and every designer created his or her own take on the jean. Denim went with the all-over tan and the big hair of Farrah Fawcett,

RIGHT A typical 1970s floor length evening dress and matching hat in navy blue moiré rayon and silk jersey, by Jean Muir.

ABOVE A sea of denim at a rock festival at Knebworth in 1979 featuring Led Zeppelin.

who along with Jerry Hall and Lauren Hutton represented an American ideal of glamour.

Yves Saint Laurent once told *Oui* magazine, "A blue jean is a classic. I believe in basics, a wardrobe for a woman that is like a man's – exactly like a blue jean – pants, jacket, raincoat, not similar in details, but in mind." [2]

GLAM FASHION
Glam rock and disco fever added colour and much needed exuberance in an uncertain world, and glam rock fashion would be integral to starting up the glitter and glamour camp and theatrical style performances of bands such as Roxy Music, David Bowie, Elton John and Marc Bolan of T.Rex. In 1972 Bowie's Ziggy Stardust became the most influential of his androgynous alter-egos and produced a fashion following like no other. From the orange, yellow and green streaked hairstyle to the loudly pattered Kansai Yamamoto jumpsuits, Ziggy had it all.

Anthony Price was well known for his stunning basque-fitted evening dresses as well as Brian Ferry's and Jerry Hall's costumes that often appeared on Roxy Music's record sleeves. The freewheeling seventies was a hotpot of style – you dressed as you pleased and from this principle a fantastic kaleidoscope of ideas came, a global fashion re-think and a host of new fashion stars.

ETHNIC AND ROMANTIC FASHION

Nova, the stylishly controversial glossy magazine published from 1965 to 1975, went ethnic. Fashion editor Caroline Baker informed her readers that "the embroidered peasant look has reached epidemic proportions in France and looks as if it will do the same here in England. Now you can find the clothes that go to make up this look without having to hunt round the antique markets."[3] You could be whom you liked. The appetite for escape fed by the movies saw every period plundered with frantic rapidity.

Ethnic dress floated from one collection to another. Thea Porter, Gina Fratini and John Bates in London all executed this type of styling, particularly the caftan, with the utmost integrity and style. Bill Gibb, or Billy Gibb as he was affectionately known, was an exciting young Scot fresh from the Royal College of Art who rapidly rose to stardom creating dramatic and highly artistic collections of appliquéd leather and flamboyantly beautiful machine-knitted designs. He frequently applied smocking and embroidery that reflected the rich colours and textures of his Celtic heritage.

ABOVE David Bowie performs on stage in 1973 at his Ziggy Stardust/Aladdin Sane tour in London in striking blue sequins and full make-up.

OPPOSITE Twiggy twirls in Bill Gibb's full-skirted peasant-style dress and knitted hat designed for her for the premiere of Ken Russell's *The Boy Friend*.

Just as the Woodstock music festival had
introduced the hippy look to America; and
Barbara Hulanicki brought a modern take on
30s glamour to Britain at Biba; so Laura Ashley
adapted Victoriana to create a fashion empire.
The Laura Ashley look proposed a young,
romantic view on 19th century dress to the
world. From her Welsh base, Laura and her
husband Bernard Ashley created a sort of idyllic
style, with advertising that depicted an image of
rural simplicity and femininity that was perfectly
timed. Her small, detailed prints on cotton; the
floor-length dresses and blouses cut close to the
body; the floppy hats, lace and ruffles found a
sweet spot amongst British traditionalists. Her
success was quick and extraordinary. She said,
"I reckon that women looked their best at the
turn of the century."

Ashley studied 18th and 19th century prints
in museum collections for her miniature floral
patterns. "No one wants to live with a design
that jumps out at them," she explained. Her
colours, too, were subdued. Ashley always
insisted that what she made was not fashion.
She said, "What we make is just an alternative
to jeans."[4]

The first American Laura Ashley shop opened
in 1974 in San Francisco. By the time of her
death in September 1985 there were over 200
Laura Ashley stores throughout the world and
the firm had 4,000 employees. Laura Ashley
preceded a generation of American designers
working in similar, restrained, classic 'lifestyle'
modes: Ralph Lauren, Calvin Klein, Anne Klein,
and Perry Ellis.

Inspired by iconic items of British country
style, such as brogues, gymslips, sturdy tweeds
and the memory of her father's gardening

mac hanging on the back of a door, in 1972 Margaret Howell tapped into British heritage with her timeless and gently androgynous clothes. Like Mary Quant before her, Margaret Howell had studied fine art at Goldsmiths. She opened her own shop at 25 St Christopher's Place, off Oxford Street.

Self-taught in the craft of dressmaking, Howell introduced soft, more relaxed tailoring for both men and women. Her thoughtfully detailed designs made in traditional fabrics such as hand-woven tweed, gabardine and the finest wools, cashmere, cotton and linen were cut into individual classics with a unique, modern twist long before we were aware of Armani or Ralph Lauren. Howell's consistently high values of design and fabrication have endured and are appreciated worldwide. Today, the company is owned by Japan's Anglobal, and Margaret Howell concentrates on what she does best – design. She continually searches for refinements to the classics using British manufacturers whenever possible. Her clothes are as sought after today by new generations of aficionados as they are by the loyal following of devotees from the seventies.

In contrast, British designer Ossie Clark, who during the 1960s was creating some of his finest work in collaboration with Celia Birtwell, reflected cosmopolitan views and a provocative take on new romanticism. David Hockney

RIGHT A 1972 design in delicate silk chiffon print with butterfly sleeves and full midi-length skirt by Ossie Clark.

OPPOSITE A flowing cream silk and chiffon floral print evening dress by Ossie Clark.

influence continued into the 1970s when he dressed the rich and famous in London, Paris and New York; designing stage costumes for people like Mick Jagger, the Beatles, Marianne Faithfull and Liza Minnelli. Percy Savage once said, "He was the Jacques Fath or Givenchy of London, with a high understanding of good workmanship. He had real respect for couture and was making clothes to a higher standard than British couture houses at the time."[5]

ZANDRA RHODES

Equally beautiful were Zandra Rhodes' innovative textiles worked into modern designs. Some of her first designs reflected her interest in Pop Art and Pucci prints. In 1969 she produced her first collection showing loose, romantic garments. Her favourite fabrics were felt and chiffon that she cut into flowing, tiered designs. Rhodes innovations included the much-copied lettuce edging on jersey, seams on the outside, torn jersey, romantic crinolines and beaded safety pins as decoration. Her unconventional and colourful prints were often inspired by travel; chevron stripes from the Ukraine and the symbols of the North American Indian, Japanese flowers, calligraphy and shells. She borrowed some of punk's hard-edged ornamentation, such as metal studs, chunky zips, brightly coloured graffiti and safety pins, to great effect.

It was with her 1977 establishment take on punk which she called *Conceptual Chic* that she made the biggest splash. She used kilts and safety pins – pre-Versace – to form a sort of embroidery, mixed with loosely drawn figures screen-printed on silk jersey, or on the newly developed Ultrasuede® fabric.

OPPOSITE A full-skirted A-line evening coat in brilliant yellow-printed wool felt with a distinctive scalloped collar, by Zandra Rhodes.

ABOVE A detail from a silk jersey dress with ball and link chain decoration from the Zandra Rhodes *Conceptional Chic* collection of 1977.

famously depicted them in his painting *Percy and Mr and Mrs Clark*. Birtwell's stylised floral prints perfectly complemented Clark's designs – sublimely feminine chiffon print dresses with daring plunge necklines and separates drifted in and out of the hippest parties. As reported by one contemporary fashion editor, "they were delicate, divine and utterly desirable."

In 1967 they signed up to design for the mass manufacturing fashion label Radley. Clark's

These striking jackets and dresses with seams on the outside or edged in blanket stitch were a surprising departure from her usual romantic, floaty chiffons.

MANOLO BLAHNIK

Working as a model in the early 70s, Manolo Blahnik's handsome face was almost as familiar as Angelica Huston's and Marie Helvin's on the pages of British *Vogue*. It was that wonderful fairy godmother, Diana Vreeland, who recognised his design talent when he showed her a portfolio of fashions and set designs; and she advised him to concentrate on designing footwear. Ossie Clark invited Blahnik to create shoes for his 1972 runway show; and an opportunity to buy the Zapata shoe brand with a loan of £2,000 ($3,200/€2,320) finally set him up.

The Zapata boutique opened in Church Street off the King's Road, where it remains today as Blahnik's flagship. Needless to say, it became and remains the most fashionable shoe shop in town. Disliking the chunky platform shoes and boots that were the mainstream footwear styling of the day, he turned his attention to the stiletto heel, so much more feminine and flattering to the leg, which has remained the brand's mainstay to this day.

THE PUNK SCENE

The punk scene was in direct opposition to glam rock, disco, romantic, traditional and ethnic styles, but like glam rock combined fashion and music movements. Punk may have started in New York's new wave music scene, but by 1975 the eclectically dressed punks had begun parading down London's King's Road.

LEFT Never out of style for some, from the spikey hair and slogan T-shirts, to stud belts and dirty denim, this group wear it all.

The punk movement expressed its anti-conformist, anti-establishment and disruptive stance through clothing and music, more visually tribal, colourful and distinctive than before. Both sexes were out to shock – they were like living graffiti with their partly-shaven or roughly cut hair, or a brightly coloured or skunk-inspired spiky mane in the centre of the head. Their bold silver jewellery included studded dog collars, safety pins, chains and studs, sometimes attached to body parts as well as to their clothes.

At the heart of this, supplying ready-made punk clothes, were Malcolm McLaren (manager of the Sex Pistols) and Vivienne Westwood, owners of the fashion store Sex. The shop's logo stood four foot high in bright pink rubber letters; needless to say, they also sold rubber and bondage fetish wear as well as Westwood's subversive designs. Her punk essentials, the bondage trousers and the T-shirts printed with provocative imagery and slogans, are increasingly valuable today at auction.

LEFT Punk princess Debbie Harry looking sultry in black-fringed leather and much copied 'Blondie' hairstyle.

European punks wore a mixed bag of styles, mostly topped off with a studded leather jacket. A signature look was the ripped T-shirt and bondage trousers with the legs strapped together behind the knees. Their clothes reflected the political argument that Ppnk was somehow countercultural and rooted in the working classes. In fact, it can be traced to sources as varied as Dadaism, the radical French art movement of the 1920s that advocated anarchy and which influenced the visual culture as well as the manifesto of punk, and to Andy Warhol's Factory, in particular the nihilistic music of the Velvet Underground and the ripped and safety-pinned clothing of Warhol 'superstar' Jackie Curtis.

For all its macho paraphernalia, punk was one youth culture that embraced women in a major way. Influential women included rock poet Patti Smith, who often wore layer upon layer of cardigans, men's shirts, and ties and big jackets all of different lengths, or loose-fitting frumpish dresses worn with heavy laced work boots. She modelled her look on the clothes and attitude of male rock stars such as Keith Richards of The Rolling Stones, Bob Dylan, Jim Morrison and Jimmy Hendrix.

Debbie Harry created a sensation early on in her career by wearing a white wedding dress when she appeared in a New York nightclub and then ripped it off when belting out *Rip Her to Shreds*. Lene Lovich put together

little girl looks from thrift shops and Fay Fife of the Rezillos and Poly Styrene of X-Ray Spex played around with ski pants and fishnet tights under sixties cast-offs like skinny rib sweaters and aggressively shiny synthetic fabrics. Siouxsie Sioux's attention-seeking hacked haircut became a key element of the 'Gothic' look. These female punk musicians were asserting their sexual freedom and poking fun at the radical feminists' denouncement of fashion.

Closer to reality was the influence of workmen's clothes often acquired at low cost from surplus stores – dungarees, collarless ex-policeman's shirts worn outside combat trousers, artist's smocks and butcher's coats trousers along with Chinese Mao jackets and government surplus accessories such as canvas cartridge bags, belts and all sorts of military paraphernalia. Antiquarius and Kensington Market in London were also Aladdin's caves for vintage 20s and 30s dress.

Working out became fashionable with the fitness craze that arrived in Europe from the west coast of America via Jane Fonda's aerobics classes and workout videos. Dance studios and gyms opened at a furious rate and the appropriate clothes followed – layers of leotards, ballerina tops, shorts, leg warmers and high-top sneakers. Flares and jeans were temporarily replaced by Lycra leggings and flounced ra-ra skirts.

Norma Kamali's brilliant interpretations of active sportswear were glamorous ra-ra skirts, wrap dresses and wide shouldered 40's style jackets, all made in sweatshirt fleece. They came in classic red, grey or black. Kamali established the OMO (on my own) Norma Kamali store in New York in 1978 and her marvelous draped and shirred 'parachute' designs, using parachute silk and drawstrings, were included in the 1977 *Vanity Fair* show at the Costume Institute, Metropolitan Museum of Art.

THE BOUTIQUES

Upmarket boutique owners aware of a demand for a wider variety of styles travelled that extra mile to find new design talent. Browns, founded in 1970 by husband and wife team Joan and Sidney Burstein on London's South Molton Street, were the most adventurous and influential leaders importing the then little-known collections of Giorgio Armani, Missoni, Sonia Rykiel, Fendi, Chloé, Comme des Garçons, Calvin Klein, Ralph Lauren, Zoran, Norma Kamali, Laura Biagiotti and others.

The fashion entrepreneur Joseph Ettedgui was born in Casablanca and came to London with his brother in the sixties. At first they opened a hair salon in London's King's Road. They soon began to sell clothing they had found in Paris, and eventually concentrated on fashion alone, establishing a new shop called Joseph in 1977. Ettedgui continued scouting Paris for more new fashion talent in the seventies, successfully launching Kenzo, then Alaïa and later Prada to appreciative British fans.

Maureen Doherty was one of those hip young Chelsea girls who Joseph Ettedgui got to know in the sixties – Maureen wore the shortest mini skirts and before tights came along used to dye her knickers to match her skirt. Joseph was impressed with the way she looked and hired her to work in his King's Road boutique and hairdressing salon.

Maureen had a brilliant eye for fashion. She soon started her own business in partnership with advertising executive, Eric Shemit. Their first shop on Sloane Square sold the Hans Metzen label. They sold slim fitting separates by this German designer and a range of fabulous crochet mini dresses in every colour imaginable. These dresses became an essential part of the 'London look.'

The Elle fashion stores in Sloane Street and New Bond Street provided a bright, sleek, white walled background for new-to-London, Italian designer brands such as Walter Albini, Basile and Cerrutti. Maureen was the first to recognise the enormous talent of Issey Miyake and Elle sold his main and diffusion collection, *Plantation*. She understood the Japanese look way before anybody else and was the first retailer to promote Yohji Yamamoto's designs in London. She was instrumental in developing and marketing Miyake's first fragrance, and persuading him to open a stand-alone store, leading to his success. It was on a trip to Milan that Maureen saw a girl wearing a short denim skirt made from vintage denim and decorated with beads and feathers. She loved it and found out it came from the huge new Elio Fiorucci store on Via Torino. Maureen knew instantly that the concept would work in London, and boldly

ABOVE Giorgio Armani fitting a model with a strapless dress with matching jacket for his spring 1978 collection.

offered to back Fiorucci and to open a store there. In 1975 Fiorucci opened on the King's Road, and was the most happening store of the decade. It introduced underground trends such as thongs from Brazil and Afghan coats, camouflage and leopard-skin prints. In 1976 a Fiorucci store opened in New York and became a celebrity spotting favourite of the disco era. Fiorucci jeans became a status symbol for the excellent cut (Fiorucci had cleverly hired a top pattern cutter from Valentino).

THE ITALIAN FASHION INDUSTRY

The Italian fashion industry had been forming slowly but surely since after the Second World War and by the seventies it had acquired a new lease on life fired with enthusiasm and a remarkable receptiveness to all forms of creativity. The Italian ability to spot trends and nurture talent were factors that attracted buyers from all over Europe.

Milan was within easy reach of Italy's wool centres, such as Florence, Prato, Valdagno and Lombardy, where cotton fabrics were also produced. It was this industrial infrastructure that financed the country's clothing manufacturing and encouraged the development of the salons specialising in female and male ready-to-wear.

In 1965 Fendi hired Karl Lagerfeld as a designer for the small family firm that sold furs and small leather goods. Nino Cerrutti, who had taken over the management of his family factory in 1950, opened the menswear boutique Hitman in Milan employing Giorgio Armani in 1964 as his assistant, passing on all the fundamentals of his craft.

Giorgio Armani left Cerrutti in 1970 and founded his own business in 1974 with his partner Sergio Galeotti. Armani challenged traditional English tailoring and deconstructed the jacket, developing his very original style. In 1975 he produced his first collection for women. Androgynous in inspiration, the line was dynamic yet understated. Like Jean Muir, Armani offered women who worked (increasingly in male-dominated fields) a restrained style that gave them a certain kind of security.

In the mid 1970s Gianni Versace moved to Milan and began working as a designer for Genny, Callaghan and Complice. The first Versace boutique opened in Milan's Via della Spiga in 1978. Husband and wife team Tai and Rosita Missoni reached the peak of their influence in the early 1970s with their ready-to-wear knitwear business. Their advertising, wonderfully evocative illustrations by Antonio Lopez, was as original as the products they sold.

Milan confirmed its position as second only to Paris as a centre of international fashion. Italian fashion was luxurious and easy to wear. It was a form of elegance that appealed to a clientele still geared towards couture. Rome was grander, of course, still favoured by the *alta moda* where Valentino, Cappucci and Schön presented couture clothes to audiences of divas, princesses and actresses.

THE INFLUENCE OF MOVIES

Movie images continued to have a powerful influence over fashion. Woody Allen's 1977 movie *Annie Hall*, starring Diane Keaton, was styled by Ralph Lauren and started a craze for masculine/feminine styles, introducing Lauren to the wider world. The soft, slightly bashed felt hat Keaton wore as she drove around New York in a convertible VW Beetle, along with midi skirt, boots and the tweed jacket, layered underneath with waistcoat, blouse and tie, was a look that appealed to masses of women. *Vogue* declared in an autumn 1976 issue,

LEFT Valentino poses with models in six of his signature red dresses and his family of pug dogs at the Valentino Museum in Italy.

OPPOSITE John Travolta struts his stuff in the famous white suit he wore on the disco dance floor in the film *Saturday Night Fever*.

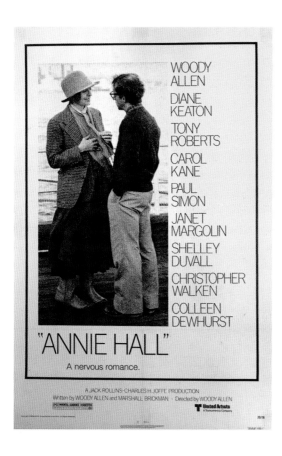

"ANNIE HALL"

A nervous romance.

"The point of this look, if you are woman enough to wear it, is not just taking the best things from a man's world and throwing in a few that are female. You need as well: ingenuity to scour the land, gain first hand information on the second-hand, leave no department unturned. An eye for quirky mixtures of colour and texture, for good cut and quality."[6]

Saturday Night Fever (1977) was the movie that captured the disco trend and catapulted it forward into the eighties. Starring John Travolta as Tony Manero, the young man from Brooklyn who lived to dance, the film was a huge commercial success based on the 1976 article in *New York Magazine* by

British writer Nik Cohn, *Tribal Rites of the New Saturday Night*. The characters that became Tony Manero and his friends were loosely based on the 1960s working class Mods who also placed great importance on music, clothes, and dancing. The Bee Gees song *Stayin Alive* remains one of the best dance sounds. A series of disco-based movies followed – *Thank God It's Friday, Roller Boogie, Can't Stop the Music* and *Fame*.

STUDIO 54

The pinnacle of New York's disco scene, Studio 54, originally a CBS radio and television studio at 254 West 54th Street in Manhattan, opened in 1977. Studio, as it came to be called, provided a public stage and fashionable parade for the disco-hungry hipsters passing through the city. Carmen D'Alessio, an ex-*Vogue* model and Valentino public relations agent, introduced owners Steve Rubell and Ian Schrager to the jet-set crowd including celebrity locals such as Roy Halston, Bianca Jagger, Liza Minnelli, Calvin Klein and Andy Warhol. At the nightclub's prime, Rubell and Schrager ruled the world of disco and became widely known for hand-selecting guests from the always-huge crowds outside, mixing beautiful 'nobodies' with glamorous celebrities in the same venue. Andy Warhol used to say that Studio 54 was a dictatorship at the door and a democracy inside. Inside everyone was a star.

One regular, Bob Colacello, recalled sitting in Studio 54's basement with Halston when Yves Saint Laurent arrived. After Halston stood up and embraced Saint Laurent, writer Truman Capote told Hugo Guinness, "You have just witnessed

LEFT Diane Keaton standing with Woody Allen on the original poster for the film *Annie Hall* where, with the help of Ralph Lauren, she developed a charming new way to dress.

OPPOSITE Studio 54 regulars designer Roy Halston, Bianca Jagger, Liza Minnelli and Jack Haley Jr. enjoy cocktails and animated conversation at the Studio

one of the great moments of the history of fashion." (As reported in *Women's Wear Daily*). The club was notorious for its drug-and-alcohol-infused hedonism and closed with one final party called *The End of Modern-day Gomorrah* on February 4, 1980.

ROY HALSTON

The 1970s offered a plethora of fashion alternatives to suit any fantasy. But if you did not want to look like a Renaisance princess, a great white hunter in top-to-toe safari gear or an Inca peasant heavily layered in clashing prints, a number of Italian designers were offering the ease of finely-tuned, carefully chosen separates. American designers had realised long ago that modern women appreciated clothes that were easy to wear and adapted to busy lifestyles but in Europe high Common Market tariffs made American imports rare and prohibitively expensive.

Roy Halston was synonymous with all things glossy, glamorous, and a little dangerous in New York. He was the first to take a less-is-more approach to clothing design. After designing hats for Jackie Kennedy, Halston became the quintessential American fashion designer of the 70s, associated with the fashionable celebrities of the day such as Liza Minnelli, Bianca Jagger, and Marisa Berenson. Halston revived the once-fashionable sweater set and sweater dress by using cashmere, argyle and matte jersey, and popularized the Japanese-made synthetic Ultrasuede®.

Typical of Halston's looks was the long cashmere dress with a sweater tied over the shoulders, silk jersey wrap skirts and turtlenecks, evening caftans, and long, slinky haltered jerseys. He was the embodiment of the designer as stylist. His empire crashed and burned when he signed a licensing agreement with J.C. Penney in 1983, infuriating his high-end retail accounts. A year later he lost the rights to his company and name but remains an inspiration to American designers to this day.

CALVIN KLEIN AND RALPH LAUREN
In September 1975, US *Vogue* pronounced, "If you were around 100 years from now and wanted a definitive picture of the American look you'd study Calvin Klein." In the early 70s Klein famously introduced his trademark jeans, which he elevated to designer status by cutting them tight and branding his name on the back pocket. A series of provocative advertisements later followed in which 15-year-old Brooke Shields cooed the line, "Nothing comes

BELOW Model and actress Lauren Hutton wears a typically glamorous halterneck evening dress by Halston.

CALVIN KLEIN

BIGGER, BOLDER, BEST

Long and Strong, Big and Bold, New Opulence, and even 'Calvin Likes it Big' were the headlines used in America to describe Calvin Klein's Fall 1981 Collection. But, whatever the adjective, this collection is his best ever. The full sweep shapes are cut with controlled ease, with sophisticated attention to detail – such as the high-roll collars on knitwear and jackets, the cape shawls on blanket coats worn with the important wide-cinched waist, belts in butter-soft draped leather over full-volume skirts in British earth tones.

All these elements make the new look come together and reflect contemporary '80s dressing at its best. The collection is made in some of the most beautiful fabrics of the season including country plaids, blanket wools dyed in Calvin Klein's special shades, leathers, suedes and fabulous prints. The silhouettes move with a feminine assertiveness in high-stepping suede boots. There are great colour combinations like rose, khaki and deep sienna for day, while for evening choose from stunning tops and skirts in silk satin charmese and mahogany silk velvet. Gold lace blouses with silk velvet Persian pants, shimmering ebony and gold ikat-printed wrap tops and pants, or simply the sensuous suede smock dresses cinched in at the waist with the 'must have' leather belt.

The essential day or night accessory is the blanket wrap or 'big sweep' that will be selling alongside the clothes in the Calvin Klein boutique. The collection includes plaids and blanket shawls in blends of wool and angora, wool and alpaca and a flannel-finished silk – all dyed to blend with the clothes. More exotic for evening are the sensuous and feminine ikat printed lamés, gold chantilly lace and a Tibetan floral and silk damask.

Calvin Klein spent longer building this collection than any before – over 6 months, selecting fabrics and colours, designing prints and ultimately creating the shapes. "I was most pleased with the dresses," said Calvin. "Coats are easy for me to design, and I've been involved with sportswear so long. But as I worked on the dresses, I saw what was happening and became very excited."

Rose/crimson blanket plaid wrap coat with sienna suede draped belt and high suede boots.

"I create change. I create moods. That's what I find really exciting when designing a collection."

Rose pink suede wrap dress with wonderful gold leaf painted belt. Jewellery by Robert Lee Morris.

Gold lace smock blouse worn with pale gold silk wrap belt and Mahogany silk velvet Persian pant. Jewellery by Robert Lee Morris. Sienna suede boots by Guido Pasquali.

Gold metallic damask smock blouse with gold metallic skirt and bronze wrap belt. Gold leaf jewellery by Robert Lee Morris.

ABOVE A fashion spread from the Browns magazine. Browns were the first boutique to import Calvin Klein's designs to London.

between me and my Calvins." This started a jeans frenzy and consumers were purchasing over 40,000 pairs a week. Klein's marketing finesse showed no bounds and by 1982 he had added his logo to boxer shorts and briefs, women's underwear and fragrances

In 1976 some experts viewed Calvin Klein as the most perceptive of US designers. He had graduated from the New York Fashion Institute of Technology and opened his house

in 1968 with the financial help of childhood friend Barry Schwartz. It did not take long before Bonwit Teller's merchandising managers recognised Klein's talent and he was honoured with a display in eight of their coveted windows showing his sleek topcoats.

After this initial success, Klein confidently designed a full line of sportswear, so-called in the sense they were the kind of clothes that work for women as uniforms do for certain sports.

RALPH LAUREN

EAST COASTING

SANTA FE TRAIL

The Classic of classics. Once clothing that expressed these attitudes was called American Ivy League. Now, creativity, sophistication, individuality and unbounded quality added, it is simply Ralph Lauren style. It's a style that's been adopted by Presidents and movie stars – it travels the test of time and always in good taste. A classic Polo blazer, soft cotton button-down shirt, striped Polo tie, hand-crafted natural leather belt and comfortable, pleated top classic trousers. All by Polo for Ralph Lauren.

On the prairie. Lauren's fabulous Navajo Fair Isle cardigan sweater worn with delicately ruffled Santa Fe blouse in sturdy blue chambray cotton and antique concho belt. A feminine counterpoint to the thick sweaters. Completing the look is a long suede skirt. A perfectionist by nature, Ralph Lauren's attention to detail, the right accessory – whether a faded bandana, scuffed boots, beaded hoop earrings, the combinations of colours like faded turquoise, sunset mauves, desert tan, the layering of elements like faded undershirt under the ruffled blouse, petticoats and leg warmers under full skirts brings a distinctive, natural charm and a down-home, easy spirit to the city streets. Photographs by Bruce Weber.

'Style, not fashion' is what Ralph Lauren stands for.

"Clothes that are fluid, soft, supple, slithery, sexy and unstuffy," as quoted by Consuelo Crespi, editor of Italian *Vogue*. It was an effortless look, the throwaway chic that Americans do so well. The key to it is the idea that separates give ultimate flexibility – each item can be mixed and matched, dressed up or down, allowing the wearer to create her own look for all hours and occasions. Klein's natural, earthy colour palette was inspired by the paintings of Andrew Wyeth and Georgia O'Keefe. His lean and elegant designs conveyed a minimalist take on understated luxury.

Ralph Lauren is perhaps the most famous of all the American designers and like Calvin Klein was born in the Bronx. With no formal design training, Lauren took business courses while working at Brooks Brothers, then as a tie salesman for Allied Stores. He established Polo by Ralph Lauren in 1968 as a menswear

ABOVE A spread from the Browns magazine. Mrs Joan Burstein, owner of Browns, also imported the Ralph Lauren collections to London, opening the first Ralph Lauren store in New Bond Street in the early 80s. The Prairie look became a fashion classic as did Ralph Lauren's Ivy look for men.

line and introduced women's clothes in 1971, beginning with cotton shirts.

The following year he expanded into a complete Ralph Lauren ready-to-wear collection. "For the thoroughbred American looking girl who really takes care of her waspish body," he created clothes that were part of a lifestyle so earthy and tweedy that he outdid the English. Think of a more sophisticated Laura Ashley. He loved Harris Tweed and British grey flannel, yet his sleek interpretations of English blazers and hacking jackets were undeniably Ralph Lauren.

Many of Hollywood's finest were his followers – Shirley MacLaine, Barbara Streisand, Diane Keaton, Lauren Bacall and Lauren Hutton were but a few. He had a huge success in 1979 with his romantic and nostalgic take on American frontier themes. The 'Prairie Look' incorporated Navaho designs knitted in jewel colours on chunky wrap jackets, worn with silver and turquoise accessories, over chambray frilled blouses and long, tiered denim or suede skirts. The look was handsome and

widely copied, a classic example of country heritage fitting perfectly into an urban lifestyle.

GEOFFREY BEENE
Geoffrey Beene was a highly respected US designer known for the quality and refined style of his collections that fell into three categories: very simple clothes, such as little wool day dresses or floor length jersey dinner dresses; sweet high-waisted dresses and ensembles based on jumpers or vests over blouses; and obvious witty looks, such as his all-sequinned, floor-length football jerseys. He went to Paris to study sketching, designing and sewing at Académie Julian. While in Paris he worked for Molyneux, master of tailoring and of the bias cut. Back in New York he set up his own company in 1963 and continued throughout the seventies.

Geoffrey Beene was one of the classiest American designers of ready-to-wear, and after studying fashion from the 14th century; he decided, "The most enduring thing, lasting

Calvin Klein Jeans

LEFT Brooke Shields declares that 'nothing' comes between her and her Calvin Klein jeans.

centuries, has been peasants clothes." His philosophy was to arrive at simplicity without looking contrived – one of the most difficult things in the world. His designs are noted for the subtle and imaginative use of colour, accenting neutrals with dashes of pure, intense shades. He often worked with unconventional textures such as designing evening dresses in grey flannel – a fabric more traditionally used for daywear.

Bill Blass, Mary McFadden, Diane von Furstenberg, Anne Klein, Perry Ellis, Willy Smith, Pauline Trigère, Oscar de la Renta, James Galanos, Cathy Hardwick, Betsey Johnson, Stephen Burrows and Liz Claiborne were all instrumental in creating and marketing so many of the fashions we know today.

AMERICAN FASHION COMES OF AGE

By 1976 American fashion had come of age after more than a century of bowing to Europe's high priest of couture. American designers won global respect as creative interpreters of a way of life; it was a rebellion and an achievement that had been building since World War II. American fashion meant healthy good looks, being in shape, well-groomed and fit for work. There was a new level of *élan* and confidence in American style that emphasised casual comfort and at the same time rediscovered the body. Designers started making versatile clothes that carried a woman through the day and past to evening. The ready-to-wear lines were virtually ageless and classless and were within the reach of most women. Misleadingly labelled "sportswear" in fact, the designation covered about 80% of the clothes women now wore.

No single designer spoke for the American look, unlike, say, Yves Saint Laurent or Kenzo Takada did for Paris fashion at this time. Yet the school of the 70s American designers ensured women always had something sassy to wear. Whether it was from the top of the class cashmere at Halston; up-market pant-suits and cocktail dresses from Oscar de la Renta and Bill Blass; Liz Claiborne's perfectly timed separates for working women or Betsey Johnson and Norma Kamali's disco bunny stretch numbers. Diane von Furstenberg had an instant hit with her practical and sexy little wrap dresses in contemporary prints and Mary McFadden began producing highly original tunic ensembles with an exotic edge.

LIZ CLAIBORNE

When Liz Claiborne started her own company in 1976 she recognized that women were entering the work force in record numbers and that it was an area that designers had not yet fully exploited. Claiborne had studied at the Fine Arts School and Painters Studio in Belgium and at the Nice Academy before returning to New York. She had always wanted to become a fashion designer and worked steadily for various companies on Seventh Avenue for nearly 20 years before starting her own business.

Claiborne's instinct was right, working women loved her separates and bought them in large numbers. She ignored the traditional industry seasons of spring and fall, opting instead for six selling periods to provide consumers with new styles every two months. Consequently, sales rocketed. The company

RIGHT Liz Claiborne in her studio in New York City.

went public in 1981 at $19 (£12/€15) per share, raising $6.1 million (£1.3/€4.9 million). After 10 years, the company was on *Fortune* magazine's list of top 500 industrial companies. It was one of the only two companies started by a woman to achieve that distinction.

In all, the seventies had been a colourful, if somewhat confusing decade for fashion and an exceptional one for feminism with the powerful female vote surely instrumental in the election of Margaret Thatcher, Britain's first woman Prime Minister.

5 Modern Legends

Big hair, big shoulders, big jewellery and big pay cheques all converged to create the nouvelle society that kicked off the 80s. This glittering world was ruled by ready cash and relentless publicity in which designers became star members, richer and more famous than most of their clients. In the UK, Margaret Thatcher was elected the first female Prime Minister, and in the US, Ronald Reagan made the world safe for the rich. The 80s saw the advent of the young, upwardly mobile professionals who were dubbed 'yuppies' by the media; their ruthless aspiration to dress as if they had 'made it' fuelling a rapidly growing market of luxury brands.

Ralph Lauren, who was ahead of the game, made that 'old money' look available to anyone who had the new money to pay

for it. In 1981 he opened his first international store in London, and in 1986 he created a convincing lifestyle destination store within his flagship Rhinelander Mansion in New York. Calvin Klein, Donna Karan, Oscar de la Renta followed suit. A popular motto heard in the eighties said it all: "If you've got it – flaunt it; and if you haven't got it – get it!"

Gianni Versace typically brought his larger than life sequined glamour to the catwalks, while Karl Lagerfeld paired leather bomber jackets with ball gowns and biker boots at Chanel. Hermès and Louis Vuitton status handbags swung proudly on logo-lovers shoulders, expanding into suburban shopping malls all over the United States and soon all over the world.

Worldwide demands for fuel made the oil-rich Arab states unfathomably wealthy and

OPPOSITE Claude
Montana's powerful
geometric shapes
dominated the early 80s
runways of Paris.

RIGHT Ralph Lauren's
flagship store in
Manhattan, New York City.

the growth in Japanese industry further widened the market for luxury fashion. The opulence and luxury of Paris couture remained best equipped to serve this new and most welcome demand, having retained a reputation for being able to produce the most intricate embroidery, the most fabulous silks and the most perfect hand finishes. The opening of trade with China and Russia was expanding the fashion industry to global proportions, prompting multiple mergers, acquisitions and alliances among companies. The eighties became the decade when fashion super-companies evolved; designers became brands, and marketing machines sold a complete lifestyle.

Women were beginning to succeed in the 1980s boardroom, and suits and dresses with strong shoulders reflected a sense of feminine power. The American television shows, *Dynasty* and *Dallas*, brought strong shoulders to the masses with the over-the-top clothing designed by Nolan Miller. Mainstream designers lost no time in creating versions of the so-called 'power-suit' that reflected sartorially the new consumerism.

Women were striding confidently into executive positions previously only held by men, even if they did slip off the sneakers for heels at the executive suite door. This trend had its origins in the New York City transport strike in 1980, when for ten days subways and buses in the five boroughs came to a screeching halt. Women were forced to consider alternative modes to get to work, from walking – hence the comfortable footwear – to cycling and roller-skating.[1] Melanie Griffith was a classic example in the movie *Working Girl* (1988)

ABOVE A glitzy dress from Nolan Miller's *Culture Collection* worn by Donna Mills. Miller designed the costumes for the popular 80s TV soap *Dynasty*.

OPPOSITE A model wears a short satin cargo dress with matching jacket and shoes, by Stephen Sprouse.

where she conveyed "a head for business and a body for sin" and wore the sexy, big-shouldered, short-skirted suit designed by Donna Karan. Power dressing, as the wide shouldered urban-style of dress was coined, continued throughout the 80s and was not limited to the boardroom. The wealthy tribe of ladies who lunched fully embraced the look. These women were often the trophy wives of bankers and industrialists who frequently occupied themselves with philanthropic endeavors. A great deal of time was spent organising fundraisers where showy appearances mattered almost as much as how much money they raised, which was considerable.

The designers they favoured did not disappoint – Valentino, Bill Blass, Oscar de la Renta, Carolina Herrera, Galanos and Adolfo. Ungaro was loved for his ruched, body-hugging print dresses. The designs of Givenchy, Thierry Mugler, Yves Saint Laurent and Karl Lagerfeld for Chanel were *de rigueur* for the must-be-seen-at lunches, cocktails and charity balls staged for good causes around the world. The difference was that these ladies had less time for couture fittings and relied more and more on the luxury ready-to-wear lines all the above designers were now obliged to produce.

Calvin Klein's sexy bias cut dresses, sensuous pastel suedes and silky metallics delighted those who shunned the obvious eighties status symbols of lavish embellishments. Stephen Sprouse, who in the seventies had designed Debbie Harry's stage clothes, launched his own collection of bright, fun clothes echoing the style of the sixties with shift dresses in day-glo colours and silk screen prints from rock videos.

LEFT Yasmin Le Bon models a minimalist-style strapless gold evening dress by Calvin Klein.

OPPOSITE A tender moment on the balcony of Buckingham Palace after the marriage of Charles, Prince of Wales and Lady Diana Spencer

The enthusiastic spending boom was played out to New Romantic music in 1981 as the world prepared for the royal wedding of Lady Diana Spencer and H.R.H. Prince Charles. It was not long before Princess Diana became the much-idolised and most glamorous member of the royal family. After her marriage those who were chosen to dress her became the stars of their day. The Emanuels made Diana's famously extravagant wedding dress and the romantic

LEFT Designer Catherine Walker, one of Princess Diana's favourites, with a group of her red carpet evening gowns.

blouse she wore for the official engagement photographs that appeared in *Vogue* magazine.

Catherine Walker of The Chelsea Design Studio became a close friend and confidante as well as the designer who created most of the iconic court and formal clothes worn by Princess Diana. Victor Edelstein, Bruce Oldfield, Jacques Azagury, Bellville Sassoon and Christina Stambolian were the designers who could also be relied upon to create appropriately grand costumes as well as work with the required discretion.

While the rich got richer, Britain was in the midst of an economic recession. Britain's bad girl, Katharine Hamnett, made the front pages of every newspaper in her biggest fashion moment when she famously shook hands with Prime Minister Margaret Thatcher at a 1984 Downing Street reception wearing sneakers and a Hamnett anti-missile T-shirt that read in huge letters on the front '58% DON'T WANT PERSHING'. Known for her slogan T-shirts, Hamnett controversially used the wearer's body as an alternative to mass media for expressing her political opinions. She also presented a new wave of textured denim treatments and finishes, including shredded denim, which reflected the country's economy and presaged the 'deconstructed' trend that would emerge later in the decade.

GAP GOES GLOBAL

Gap opened in London and then worldwide, offering a new way to shop. The company had started out as a discount jeans store in California in the sixties. The founders Donald and Doris Fisher had built the company to corporate success but realised they needed a new identity and called in the brilliant merchandiser Millard 'Mickey' Dexler as president. He swiftly created a large in-house design staff to develop a line of clothes beyond jeans that would be casual and simple. Made of natural fibres, the look was informal but classic.

Gap's stores were revamped and the new interiors were fresh and bright in neutral grey and white with shelves of neatly folded clothing in a range of fashionable colours. The clothes came in a range of sizes to fit young and old at relatively low cost. And when Drexler launched the "Individuals of Style" advertising campaign, a series of black and white photographs of both famous and unknown subjects by a team of celebrated photographers stressing iconic style rather than the company, Gap came to mean good taste of a more formal variety, and the brand name become a generic part of the basic wardrobe. They were also one of the first chains astute enough to sense a need for stylish children's clothes and baby wear, launching Gap Kids and Baby Gap to cover the basic clothing needs of all generations.

THE DESIGNER DENIM
MARKET EXPANDS

In the 80s people didn't wear just any old blue jeans. They went straight for designer denim. Although Gloria Vanderbilt had started the designer jean ball rolling in the mid seventies,

it was Calvin Klein who had created a denim phenomenon with his provocative advertising campaign. Then Jordache introduced their tight, sexy fashion-forward jeans to the United States from their European base. Posters and TV commercials went that bit further featuring sparsely clad models in athletic poses. One commercial entitled *You got the Look*, was even spoofed on *Saturday Night Live* by Gilda Radner with special guest Andy Warhol proving the ultimate power of cleverly placed advertising.

Jordache soon grew into a global brand with over 60 international licensees applying the Jordache name to countless items such as eyeglasses, luggage, bedding, cosmetics and fragrance – even babies – diapers and sales grew to more than $600 million (£370 million/€480 million). French Moroccan brothers George, and Maurice Marciano followed suit. They had moved to California from France in 1977 and in 1981 launched their jeans company, Guess?. Start-up money came from the Nakash family, owners of the Jordache Empire.

Guess? Jeans first style in the new 'stone-washed' denim was a three-zipper design called *Marilyn*. Bringing a touch of Hollywood glamour to the east coast, exclusive stockists Bloomingdales in New York quickly sold out. Guess?, with their distinctive triangular branding, introduced a series of award winning black and white advertisements in 1985 debuting models who were later to become prominent members of the 'Supermodel' clan: Claudia Schiffer, Eva Herzigova and Laetitia Casta.

Many more jeans brands appeared during the 80s and took their fair share of the ever-

expanding market, including Diesel, Tommy Hilfiger and Versace. Even the notorious Studio 54 nightclub launched a range with a slogan that pronounced, "Now everyone can get into Studio 54". Every designer who was anybody had a denim range to his or her name.

If denim needed further endorsement of its youthful edginess, two of the most iconic female pop music artists of the decade, Cyndi Lauper and Madonna, chose this humble cloth to project the perfect stage image to their massive young audiences. So it was not surprising that the new editor of American *Vogue*, Anna Wintour, should choose a pair of denim jeans for her first cover in November 1988. With magpie chic she had selected a Christian Lacroix bejeweled sweater to top off this modern, freewheeling image. An image that demonstrated it was OK to mix the basic with luxury; to pick clothes from more than one source whether it was from a thrift shop or the couture.

VIVIENNE WESTWOOD

Meanwhile, back in London Vivienne Westwood had abandoned bondage, punks and seditionaries for pirates. The 1981 *Pirate Collection* was a romantic's dream and her first runway show at Olympia. London's young rebels and fashion editors soon took up the Pirate look with enthusiasm, creating great photographic images. These were colourful, fantasy clothes inspired by 17th century pirates that caught the imagination of both the fashion crowd and the street-chic club scene, in which Boy George played an increasingly influential part. The frills and furbelows, pirate shirts, sashes and swash-buckling breeches came in opulent brocades and darkly striped madras, edged with broidery Anglaise and accessorised with red and white chain print sashes and thick cotton stockings. Feet were adorned with baggy-round-the-ankle flat heel boots. Hair ringlets, gold teeth and tricorn hats were optional. It was frivolous and fun and hit the right spot, elevating Westwood to worldwide fame.

The following season more history appeared on Westwood's catwalk in the guise of *Savages*. She mixed historical garments with ethnic ideas; there was body paint, mud plastered into hair and oversized hats. Westwood transferred to Paris in 1982, at first showing in the genteel Angelina tearooms on the Rue de Rivoli (quite a shock for the locals who peered in through the large glass windows at the fantastic scene staged on an elevated catwalk inside). This time the theme was *Buffalo Girls*. Brassieres were worn over sweaters, hooded sweatshirts with tailoring – all in muddy

LEFT The distinctive triangular Guess? jeans label placed on the back pocket of denim jeans.

OPPOSITE From her iconic 1980 *Pirate Collection*, an ensemble complete with tricorn hats and flat suede boots, by Vivienne Westwood.

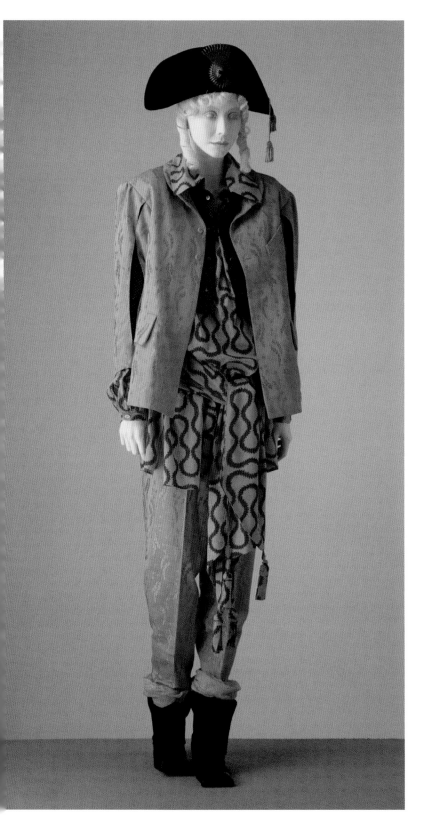

and camouflage colours – ahead of America's grunge look a few years later.

Westwood, who was never afraid of experimentation, combined historical research with her intuition to create forward-looking ideas that have often been ridiculed, but have an uncanny history of being picked up by the mainstream years later. The *Mini Crini* of her solo spring '84 collection at the Carrousel de Louvre, where she was permitted to show with the French prêt-à-porter designers, was a case in point. The *Crini* was a return to traditional fit where the emphasis was placed on the hip and represented a radical change from the popularity of the big shoulder. Hooped puffball skirts inspired by Victorian crinolines in a giant polka dot print went with tailored jackets and platform shoes. The world of fashion wondered what she would think of next – it was Harris Tweed, which she reintroduced into high fashion with fine knitwear, twin sets, and pearls, as well as rocking-horse platform shoes complete with Statue of Liberty corsets.

Experimental design came from unexpected places in the eighties. Apart from the surrealism, René Magritte and chocolate, Belgium was not known for its contributions to culture until a group of young, avant-garde fashion designers emerged from Antwerp's Royal Academy of Fine Arts. They called themselves The Antwerp Six and presented a distinct, radical alternative vision for fashion during the 1980s that later established Antwerp as a notable location for fashion design. Walter Van Beirendonck, Ann Demeulemeester, Dries van Noten, Dirk Van Saene, Dirk Bikkembergs and Marina Yee set off in their hired truck for London Fashion Week

in 1988 with their deconstructionist collections. The other Belgian making waves was Martin Margiela, who set up his own label in 1984 developing a distinctively downbeat style, turning fashion, literally, inside-out.

GIORGIO ARMANI

The prowess of Italy's designers had, in the meantime, accelerated massively, and the world's press and buyers eagerly descended upon Milan for the well-organised round of biannual ready-to-wear shows. Armani became the leader; with a background in menswear and a wide knowledge of fabric technology, his jackets were the most sought after of the decade.

Giorgio Armani made his mark with a radical reassessment of the male suit jacket. He re-examined it in terms of structure, weight, the way different parts were assembled and the materials of which it was made. With this analytical process completed, he developed his very individual, entirely modern style.

From the beginning the line was urban, dynamic and understated, and undoubtedly androgynous in inspiration. Armani offered a restrained style that gave women a sense of security, authority and femininity; and men a sense of elegant shape combined with a softer structure. Armani had been described as "the Chanel of the eighties." Without doubt,

OPPOSITE Playful *Mini-Crini* skirt in a bold polka dot pattern from the 2001 collection shown in Paris, by Vivienne Westwood.

LEFT Giorgio Armani's 1985 suit option of collarless jacket with broad shoulders and fluid wool trousers.

an Armani suit, whether for woman or man, became shorthand for success. Armani launched Emporio Armani, the secondary arm of his label, in 1981, making his brand of contemporary dress more affordable and democratic.

By 1987 Armani was a highly desirable luxury brand and in just over a decade the company's turnover was £350 million ($560 million/€406 million). Never complacent in his success, by 1988 Armani sensed women were looking for a softer look, and all hailed his spring collection as a triumph. Nina Hyde of *The Washington Post* wrote, "At Armani, where some of the best jackets for men and women have been masterminded over the

years, the changes are in more than length. In his spring collection for women the armhole of the jackets was smaller, the sleeves narrow and the shoulders padded in a natural way."[2]

Her report went on to describe the way Armani had shown both long and short jackets in very soft fabrics, without linings, almost like sweaters, with very narrow lapels. He had made several jackets with elbow-length sleeves shown with blouse sleeves poking through from them. "People often roll up the sleeves of my jackets, so I thought I would simply cut them that way," he said.

There was no such thing as a simple straight skirt in Armani's collections. "People

LEFT An exhibition of Giorgio Armani fashion designs at the Royal Academy, Burlington Gardens, London, in 200

OPPOSITE A richly eclectic style in gold and brown silks from the autumn/win 1989 collection of Romeo Gigli.

already have those," he says. And so he put lettuce edges on some, and made others that were shorter in the front than in the back. The refinement and lightness of his clothes was totally liberating.

ROMEO GIGLI

Romeo Gigli was the Italian artisan who expressed his version of romance in a new, sensuous and individual way in the eighties. Like so many other fashion designers before him, he had originally trained as an architect but his call to fashion came in 1983 with his first showing in Milan. His interpretation of eighties' femininity was that of a flower girl rather than the sharp-suited executive the rest of Milan was promoting.

Inspired by a variety of cultural or ethnic dress, Gigli created a signature look that celebrated the feminine, but did not sexualise the wearer, rather like his hero, Yohji Yamamoto. He offered unstructured clothes in diaphanous or plain matte stretch fabrics which skimmed the figure. He liked the empire waistline, bare shoulders and long, slim sleeves.

Gigli grew up surrounded by antiquarian books; both his father and grandfather dealt in books of the 15th and 16th centuries, so it was not surprising he frequently returned to the Renaissance period for inspiration. In 1989 he decided to show in Paris, still the centre of fashion and the biggest international market place. Produced by Zamasport, his autumn/winter *Byzantine* collection was sensational. From the first layer of close-fitting jersey separates and dresses teased into

folds and drapes in darkly rich jewel colours; to the opulent gold-infused silks, satins and damask fabrics of the top layers, the body was cocooned in colour, texture and light.

Glamorous and ethereal at the same time, Gigli combined literary influences and ethnic decoration to illustrate contemporary trends. After success and a diffusion line in the 1990s, he was finally unable to balance the demands of international distribution and lost the rights to his own name in 2004.

FRANCO MOSCHINO

Franco Moschino was the self-styled joker and bad boy of the fashion pack. He loved breaking the rules and built his very successful business on irony – his tongue was very much in his cheek when he called his labels COUTURE! and CHEAP & CHIC. Moschino started as an illustrator working for a variety of designers. His clothes were beautifully made, but he remained the prankster and provocateur. He loved to have fun with a play on words appliquéd on jackets, such as "Waist of Money," "Fashion is full of Chic" or "Ready to Where."

GIANNI VERSACE

Throughout the 1980s Gianni Versace was known for the striking colour-drenched prints, lavish embroideries and new technical fabrics he used to flatter a woman's body. He was instrumental in promoting the 'supermodels' as the group of highly paid girls who continuingly endorsed his glamorous image, though

Versace's early collections were thought sexy to the point of vulgarity – plunging necklines and miniskirts, sheath dresses and gaudy accessories. Versace did not care; it was his vision of loveliness and it sold. He worked leather into marvelous body-skimming shapes using studs and lace and became known for his shimmering silver chain mail dresses that draped lightly and sexily on the body like a living, free-moving sculpture.

Versace broke new ground by the restyling of basic sportswear clothing into luxurious materials and exploring contrasting textiles and patterns. He used Jazz Age patterns in brilliant colours on second-skin catsuits ingeniously embroidered with threads of beads by the French house of Lesage. He depicted motifs from the ancient world with embroidery and silk prints to express the opulence of his ideas, always with wit and modernity, creating a unique identity and a massive fortune for his house.

For all his achievements it was what is often referred to as "that dress", the barely there long black dress made from pieces of silk and Lycra fabric, held together at the sides with gold safety pins with a wide, open neckline, revealing Elizabeth Hurley's pert breasts, that is perhaps his best known creation. Lent to unknown actress and model Hurley from the press cupboard to accompany Hugh Grant to a film premiere, it caused a media frenzy and appeared on every front page the next day, setting up Hurley's future career and proving further that by subverting tradition, exploring the limits of what is sartorially achievable, and going a few steps further Versace created his own luxurious kingdom.

THE SPECTACLE OF FASHION

Paris, despite increasing competition, was staging bigger and better fashion shows than anywhere else with lasers, loud music, choreography and spotlights. The schedules were organized as a group by Didier Grumbach at the Fédération Française de la Couture, du Prêt-à-Porter des Couturiers et des Créateurs de Mode, and right-hand woman, Andrée Putman. A former ballet dancer, Thierry Mugler, was famous for his spectacular fashion shows which showcased his galactic ideas and futuristic lines: the spiraled shoulders, clenched waists and gladiator accessories that looked like science fiction fantasies, especially on his favourite model, Jerry Hall. He was the first designer to invite the public to view one of his shows in Paris, where the audience numbered more than six thousand.

Designers were entertaining on a grand scale, hosting dinners and weddings and parties at their homes or paying for parties for the masses in the new, trendy clubs. Fashion shows had become social entertainment events and people clamored to attend, so much so that security guards were brought in to check invitations at the door. Many journalists without seat numbers were left to seek out the appropriate colour of felt tipped pen, star,

OPPOSITE Liz Hurley with Hugh Grant wearing the infamous black and gold safety pin evening dress by Gianni Versace for the premiere of the film *Four Weddings and a Funeral*.

RIGHT Intergalactic fantasies reign at Thierry Mugler's autumn/winter 1984 runway show; pale yellow fur evening jacket edged in silver.

LEFT Claude Montana's evening dress unfolds like an exotic flower in blue velvet, satin and feathers; from his autumn/winter 1982 collection.

stick-on circle etc. in order to gain entry to the show in a dignified way – anything to avoid the embarrassment of standing at the back or even worse, standing outside until the bitter end!

Claude Montana was famous for going that extra mile, producing shows reminiscent of a Las Vegas spectacular. His Amazonian heroines posed like fashion plates as they prowled the catwalk to loud operatic music, the world's press photographers now grouped at the end of the runway eager to capture their favoured models' best pose under the spotlight. Indeed, the eighties was the perfect platform for Montana's brief career that ended in 1989 through lack of financial backing. His extraordinary theatrical presentations will be remembered for their fearlessly bold shapes, clear primary colours and extraordinary hats by master milliners Stephen Jones and Jean Barthet; along with Didier Malige's amazing geometric hairstyles. After being so typical of eighties excess, Claude Montana took charge of Maison Lanvin from 1990 to1992, where he proved he could also be a top rate couturier.

THE POWER OF THE SUPERMODELS

In an increasingly crowded market advertisers were a powerful force, especially in magazine publishing. As circulation figures declined and the Internet was fast becoming a new source of communication, the major fashion houses could, and very often would, withdraw their advertising if editorial representation was not included. In order to survive, publishing directors had no choice but to comply, and featured the most desired advertisers in the editorial pages. Survive they did; the established glossies became swollen with luxury brand advertising,

using the best photographers and the band of now familiar faces and perfect bodies of the supermodels. Advertising dominated the pages and competed with fashion editorials to gain global recognition. In some cases designers would launch their own publications, like Comme des Garçon's bi-annual cultural magazine *Six*, launched in 1988 to reinforce their cultural niche in the market.

There was also a shift in power among those responsible for creating these photographic fantasies. Whereas photographers were at the top of the tree financially in the sixties, twenty years later it was the models who were calling the shots and earning hundreds of thousands of dollars. Top models have always earned good money as their careers are usually brief; and they often became celebrities. If they were lucky enough to become very celebrated, as Lauren Hutton did after she became an actress, they began receiving credits alongside the photographer on the pages of *Vogue* and *Harper's Bazaar*.

Landing highly paid contracts with cosmetic companies was the reward for editorial success. The eighties saw a whacking 400% rise in model fees; the supermodels included Claudia Schiffer, Cindy Crawford, Naomi Campbell, Christy Turlington, and Linda Evangelista, who was quoted as declaring "We don't wake up for less than $10,000 a day." These new, young, beautiful and sometimes precocious tycoons often refused to appear alongside another model on the same page. In some cases they walked off the set refusing to wear the clothes; and some thought nothing of cancelling at the last moment if a better job came along.

REI KAWAKUBO AND
YOHJI YAMAMOTO

In contrast to the hedonistic mood that
surrounded the couture, two new faces
appeared on the scene in Paris: the Japanese
designers Rei Kawakubo (Comme des
Garçons), and Yohji Yamamoto. They both
arrived in Paris in 1981, showing their first
collections in 1982. Their loosely layered and
unusually cut clothes were shocking at first,
and difficult for the mainstream to understand.
The fabrics were usually In drab, textured and
hand-dyed colours such as black, inky blue and
grey. Kawakubo sent models down the catwalk
wearing rags in their hair, no make-up and what
looked like a bruised bottom lip. The clothes
seemed ragged and to have no particular
shape. The models were not the usual catwalk
girls, but regular photographic models like those
Kenzo first started to use in the seventies.

Women's Wear Daily dismissed this first
collection under the headline "Intellectual Bag
Ladies", writing that the look "was inspired
by the residents of railroad stations and bus
depots" and called it "Terminal Fashion." But for
all *WWD*'s witty (if a touch sarcastic) headlines,
Rei Kawakubo quickly found a following and
spearheaded a new movement, popularly
known as 'deconstructivism'. Deconstructivist
garments were generally black and were
designed to be oversized or shrunken, or to
appear as if inside-out, with uneven hemlines
and exposed seams and slashes.

RIGHT The 1982 'bag lady' look from
Rei Kawakubo for Comme des Garçons;
a lace knit sweater over jersey top and
cotton jersey skirt.

The arrival of the Japanese designers in Paris had coincided with a general renaissance in the field of retail architecture, graphic design, and advertising; and Kawakubo's minimalist philosophy coupled with her obsessive attention to detail in the subtle manipulation of fabrics catapulted her onto the international fashion market. Her designs were rapidly adopted as a kind of uniform for those working in the creative professions. To wear Comme des Garçons or (at that time) Yohji menswear, was to proclaim membership to a cool sect.

Yohji Yamamoto eventually became one of the most influential and enigmatic designers of our time. He challenged traditional notions of fashion by designing garments that seemed oversized or unfinished; he played with ideas of gender or used fabrics not normally used in fashionable attire such as felt or neoprene. His ideas and developments consequently paved the way for a more lateral, less conventional approach to fashion design for many designers.

One fan of this radical minimalism was Joan Burstein of the Browns boutiques in London, whose shrewd business choices and contemporary style have since become legendary. She said at the time, "The most radical change in fashion in recent times has been the advent of the Japanese designers, they have created a new feeling unrelated to anything else that has gone before. I find it quite fascinating the way it has taken off. I wear it

LEFT A serious looking grey flannel trouser suit by Japanese designer, Yohji Yamamoto, dated 1982.

and love wearing it; I have a dress and coat that I wear constantly... I think it is a sensation of a form of freedom that their designers manage to achieve; there is nothing structured around you except a waistband and it gives women sensuality and a fascination of fabric. Their fabrics are never flat, always textured."[2]

Browns boutique in London's South Molton Street were the first to discover many designers who have since become household names. It was Joan Burstein who in 1984 bought John Galliano's entire graduation collection called *Les Incroyables* (the unbelievables), inspired by a group of young French nonconformist dandies who expressed sympathy with republican ideals through revolutionary sartorial excesses. Galliano was the star pupil of his year at Central Saint Martin's School of Art where his interest in the way that young children learned how to dress, at first putting their legs through sleeves, arms through necklines and closing buttons at random, led to his abstract forms of twisted fabrics and improvised details such as coins and corks for buttons.

DONNA KARAN AND HER SEVEN EASY PIECES

In 1985 Donna Karan introduced her new range of *Seven Easy Pieces,* a concise collection in a deeply luxurious navy blue wool jersey that sensuously draped and wrapped to form seriously feminine shapes, yet could be worn respectably on most occasions. There was a wrap jacket, several different 'bodies' to go underneath, a wrap skirt, catsuit and dress. All were designed to be flexible and take the wearer in style from office to dinner; and it was hard to resist buying the lot, as all wardrobe needs would be taken care of in one sweep.

Karan had taken over as head designer at Anne Klein when Klein died in 1974. In 1984 she left the firm to start her own business "to design modern clothes for modern people." Karan's aim was to dress women in comfort – to liberate them from the confines of 80s' power suits. Karan, like McCardell before her, understood the variations in the feminine form and through the fabric that she chose, ensured that women were flattered by the shapes she created.

In the press release for her winter 1988 collection, Karan said, "It's not just colour but also shape that shines through this season. A shape once again that relies on my use of stretch. A new more gently sculpted figure is revealed beneath the moulding and draping of fabrics. Fabrics that have a surface interest all of their own: bouclé, suede, mohair, velvet, satin, silk crêpe and knits for evening. It's a look where the issue of length is almost irrelevant. The length is what shape and proportion dictate, not the arbitrary or random decision of the designer."[3]

Karan's advertising campaigns reinforced the power and glamour the company had gained and by 1992 "In Women We Trust" was the banner showing the beautiful and believable model Rosemary McGrotha in the role of female US president in pinstripes and pearls. Perhaps this idea had inspired President and Hillary Clinton to both wear Donna Karan suits for his inauguration in January 1993. In 1988 DKNY was created for the

OPPOSITE Elegant navy jersey body, wrap skirt and long jacket, by Donna Karan, photographed during a fashion show in New York.

younger market; today Karan's company is a lifestyle brand producing menswear, jeans, accessories, hosiery, fragrances and cosmetics. The company was sold in April 2010 to French luxury conglomerate LVMH for almost $210 million (£133 million/€168 million) in cash.

ZORAN

While fashion in the 1980s was all about the show, many wealthy women in society prefer fashion that is anonymous, except to those in their select circle. Zoran Ladicorbic, who goes by his first name, has grown rich by selling minimalist clothes that have changed little in 30 years. He started his collection in 1976 and devised a formula that revolved around the functionality of a few good shapes that were the basis for a wardrobe. Like Balenciaga, he figured out long ago that the true customers of expensive clothes were wealthy women over 35, who led active professional and social lives and who were not fashion victims. Zoran's clothes flattered mature women and were comfortable; to this day he remains the quiet secret of many of the world's most elegantly dressed women.

Like his colour palette, a range of neutral shades, Zoran's silhouettes vary little from season to season but are always made in the most luxurious fabrics, some of which even the French couture are reluctant to use because of the extraordinary high cost. Double silk georgette, Tasmanian wool, six-ply cashmere, and silk gazar are used generously for the simple shapes that come without sharp shoulder pads or linings, buttons, zips, or embellishments of any kind. The collection is based on square and rectangular shapes in a choice of four or five solid colours – a uniform, in effect. Zoran's strict (and some would say arrogant) code of personally monitoring when and to whom he is selling has maintained his aura of exclusivity over the years.

AZZEDINE ALAÏA

Azzedine Alaïa started showing his collections in 1981 and hit a sensational high note with his body-hugging garments. Perfectly timed, they were snapped up by women whose bodies were freshly toned from the aerobic studios. He used synthetic fabrics such as Lycra creatively

LEFT Azzedine Alaïa's models applaud followin a show in his Paris studio All dressed in body-hugging jewel coloured satin evening dresses.

to achieve his second-skin designs. Alaïa was
soon dubbed 'The King of Cling' by the fashion
media and worshipped by models, private
clients and fashion devotees alike. Indeed,
Alaïa's models gladly worked for him in return
for the clothes they wore. The no-compromise
shapeliness of his designs were undoubtedly
liberating yet blatantly sexual.

Alaïa came from a farming family in
Tunisia. He had a twin sister who loved fashion
and inspired his love of couture – so much so
that he lied about his age to get himself into
the local École des Beaux-Arts in Tunis, where
he began studying sculpture and gained
valuable insights into the human form. Alaïa
moved to Paris in 1957 where he worked as
a dressmaker's assistant. He worked at Dior

as a tailleur, at Guy Laroche and with Thierry
Mugler until he opened his first atelier in a tiny
apartment on the rue de Bellechasse in 1977.
For almost 20 years he dressed some of the
world's most celebrated beauties from this
tiny apartment, from Greta Garbo to Helene
de Rothschild.

Alaïa moved to larger premises in the
Marais district of Paris, where he produced his
first ready-to-wear collection and found support
from French magazine editors and designers.
While walking down Madison Avenue in New
York wearing one of Alaïa's first leather coats,
Andrée Putman was stopped by a Bergdorf
Goodman buyer who asked her what she was
wearing. Alaïa was soon selling to Bergdorf's
and eventually opened his own boutiques in
New York and Beverly Hills. In 1984 his talent
was recognised and the French Ministry of
Culture voted him Best Designer of the Year
and Best Collection of the Year at the Oscars
de la Mode in a memorable event where
singer Grace Jones affectionately carried the
diminutive designer in her arms on stage!

When Alaïa's twin sister died in the mid-
nineties, he became reclusive and presented
his small collections to just a handful of chosen
industry names in his studio; but in 2000 he
signed a partnership with the Prada Group.
Working with Prada for seven years, he
eventually bought back his house and brand
name. Following this the Richemont Group
(Cartier, Van Cleef, Net-à-Porter) took a stake
in Alaïa's fashion house but have allowed
him complete freedom. He still chooses to
show only when he has something really new
to reveal, and in his own time frame, thus
remaining mysterious, exclusive and expensive.

JEAN PAUL GAULTIER

France, not known for radical design, had an ace card with Jean Paul Gaultier, who was dubbed their *enfant terrible*. Today, as he approaches 60, he is as irreverent as ever and one of the world's most respected French-born couturiers. In 1970, at the impressionable age of 18, Jean Paul Gaultier became Pierre Cardin's assistant after impressing him with his sketched ideas. He then worked with Jacques Esterel followed by two years at Jean Patou, first with Michel Gomez and then with Angelo Tarlazzi, before returning to manage the Pierre Cardin boutique in Manila.

On his return to Paris he began making electronic jewellery with his partner, Francis Menuge. He started to present his own fashion in 1978, but it was not until 1981 that the editors of *Elle* and *Marie Claire* recognised him for his mastery of tailoring – particularly the long, wide-shouldered jackets with a distinctive tab on the back that were always in his collections. Gaultier subverted the clichés of masculinity and femininity. In 1985 he introduced the controversial man-skirt that, allegedly, sold more than three thousand pieces.

Having been labeled the *enfant terrible* from the start of his career Gaultier has always managed somehow to live up to it. His idea of beauty is not the stereotyped image; he sees beauty in different things, in different types of people. People he sees on the street often appear on his runway. Sometimes he brings the runway to the street, presenting his highly entertaining fashion shows in shopping arcades, transforming them into street theatre. He often gives the impression that he is ridiculing both

ABOVE Madonna performing on stage at Wembly Stadium on the *Blonde Ambition Tour* in pink satin corset, by Jean Paul Gaultier.

men and women by dressing them almost in the mood of a Fellini movie, but his work is always underpinned by superb workmanship and historical knowledge. He frequently turns ordinary things like shredded denim or a tuxedo into a thing of beauty with a witty and unexpected twist. His signature piece is the Breton stripe sailor's jersey, which under his creative direction can turn up on the runway as anything from a ball gown to a brassiere. He is possibly most famous, though, for the conical bra he designed for Madonna's stage appearances in the 1990s.

CHRISTIAN LACROIX

Couture grandeur was further endorsed by the first major posthumous exhibition of Cristobal Balenciaga's work at the Musée des Tissus in Lyons, resulting in the revival of the puff-ball skirt. Ungaro, who used to work as Balenciaga's assistant, was one of the first to pick up on the idea. Then Christian Lacroix sent shock waves through the world of haute couture in 1986 with his dramatic and theatrically brilliant couture collection for the long-forgotten house of Jean Patou.

Lacroix came to Paris from Arles in the south of France where he studied art history. While French couture was suffering another slump, Lacroix knew there would always be a small, wealthy and discerning clientele for exciting and exquisitely made clothing; he catered to this sector of the market. Emerging (rather like Christian Dior) from near anonymity, this 26-year-old renegade introduced 'the pouf', a frothy, frilly extravagance of a dress; and fashion went mad. *People* magazine called his

spring/summer 1986 collection "a madcap mix of elegance and razzle-dazzle." And *The Sunday Times* were ecstatic: "Vive Lacroix! There's been nothing like it in 25 years," they proclaimed.

A little more than a year before, Vivienne Westwood had provided plenty of inspiration with the launch of the *Crini*. Lacroix had elaborated on the idea to suit the mood of the moment. His ideas, knowingly borrowed, were fun and fantastic. He created wildly photogenic wide-based skirts, pert little cocktail dresses that had a traditional front with a small bustle at the back, and wildly luxurious ball gowns. He was not afraid to mix the sharpest colours, textures and patterns, and used decorative embroidery lavishly. Many of his designs echoed the traditional costumes of the Camargue and were always quintessentially French. Lacroix was considered the toast of Paris throughout the eighties, despite the stock market crash in 1987, because he had the free spirit to take couture to a new level – one less serious than before.

In 1987 he abruptly left Patou after an offer he could not refuse. Christian Lacroix Couture was launched under the umbrella of Financière Agache, a French company that owned other fashion houses including Dior and textile manufacturer, Boussac. Bernard Arnault, the owner of Financière Agache, was in the process of acquiring LMVH, the French multinational luxury goods conglomerate. As Brigit Foley wrote in *WWD*, "When Lacroix signed with Agache, his long time associate Jean-Jacques Picart called the deal a contract for life." But the house never made money, even after launching

a perfume, *C'est la vie*, and a diffusion line, *Bazaar*. While his name will be forever associated with the madcap fashion publicist, Edina, portrayed by the British comedian Jennifer Saunders in the TV series, *Absolutely Fabulous*; Lacroix's frou-frou style did not sit well in the minimalist nineties.

Sadly, in 2005 LVMH sold the Lacroix brand to the Florida based Falic Group, a concern ill-suited to the highly specific, highly emotional world of fashion. The couture and ready-to-wear collections were soon shuttered. Christian Lacroix SNC is now a licensing operation in which the designer has no part.

KARL LAGERFELD

Of all the designers who made an impression on the 1980s, it is perhaps Karl Lagerfeld who stands above the crowd. He is the powerhouse who in 1983 was appointed design director of couture, ready-to-wear and accessories at Chanel. He was already an established star and a notorious workaholic with regular appearances at the end of the catwalk at Chloe, Fendi and the Italian firm Alma. At the then-dusty Chanel, Lagerfeld embarked on an unparalleled and ongoing run of successes. He went along with Coco Chanel's basic concept that "individual items of clothing are not as important as what they are accessorized with and how they are worn". She translated and communicated a total look. Karl Lagerfeld did exactly that; he picked up random ideas and styled them to suit himself.

LEFT Christian Lacroix surrounded by his models and muse, Marie Seznec (fourth from right), at his first couture show in 1988, the year he won the Golden Thimble Award.

Lagerfeld produced his first couture collection for Chanel in 1983, breathing new life into the house with his unbounded energy and imagination. He injected a youthful sophistication to the brand without destroying Coco's finest achievements. The pearls, the gilt chain belts and necklaces, the little tweed suit, the elegant two-tone shoes and, of course, the camellia and black satin bow; all became accessories to the newly proportioned designs that reflected his own contemporary ideas, worn by his hand-picked Chanel muse of the moment. These included the aristocratic Inès de la Fressange, and then supermodels, Linda Evangelista, Claudia Schiffer, Stella Tennant, Karen Elson and Devon Aoki. Lagerfeld had found a shrewd way to promote a model's image, his own, and Chanel's at the same time. To this day Lagerfeld still puts in an amazing 16-hour day and is at the top of his game, reinventing his personal style as and when it is needed.

Lagerfeld made sure he fulfilled a childhood dream when he joined Chanel. One of the first changes he made was to take over the photography of his own publicity and advertising campaigns. "Fashion, which is my own true form of expression, has always been and still remains a pretext for taking photos. It is a regular incentive to photography, and the connection between the two is perfectly logical," he declared in the 1990 edition of his book of portraits dedicated to Eric Pfrunder.

RIGHT Inès de la Fressange wearing a Chanel body suit and jacket edged in gold; part of an autumn/winter 1989 collection.

YVES SAINT LAURENT

Despite the new competition edging in from all directions during the 1980s, Yves Saint Laurent continued his strokes of genius. Ever since the hugely successful Mondrian dress of 1965, Saint Laurent found raw material for his imagination in the work of artists. From Bakst's designs for Diaghilev's *Ballets Russes* in 1976 to the Picasso-inspired cocktail dresses of winter

1979, YSL paid homage to the work of artists he admired by breaking down the barriers between art and fashion, much in the spirit of Andy Warhol.

Saint Laurent's evident love of contemporary art lies just below the surface of his designs. His spring/summer 1988 couture collection paid homage to Braque and Van Gogh in fabulous embroideries brilliantly transferred onto textiles by the legendary François Lesage. Yves Saint Laurent's art-inspired collections presented the embroiderer with many challenges; but each time the result was a triumph.

As a Leo, Saint Laurent loved gold and used it lavishly. In his clever way he often took an everyday item such as the trench coat or sailors' pea jacket, and transformed it into the ultimate glamour piece by making it in butter soft gold leather, cashmere or brocade. "I love gold, a magical colour, for the reflection of a woman. It is the colour of the sun,"[4] he told Laurence Benaim. Saint Laurent's painterly eye for colour was daring, especially when he mixed four or even five strong jewel colours into one costume.

A woman was confident that she looked good and could get on with the business of enjoying herself when wearing an Yves Saint Laurent suit or coatdress, whether in the work place or out and about. The distinctive cut of the jacket defined by the sure definition of the shoulder line, the perfect lay of the collar and the way the waist gently curved, the length of

LEFT Yves Saint Laurent's evening jackets from the summer 1988 haute couture collection inspired by Van Gogh's iris and sunflower designs, embroidered by the legendary François Lesage.

the skirt which fell directly to the most flattering length allowed for maximum femininity yet retained an air of authority.

The Saint Laurent show at New York's Metropolitan Museum of Art in 1983, curated by Diana Vreeland, was the first exhibition the Costume Institute had dedicated to the work of an individual living designer and confirmed Saint Laurent as one of the world's most important couturiers of our time. Asked why she selected him for that show, Vreeland replied, "I selected Yves because for 26 years he has kept women's clothes on the same high level". Vreeland added that "if you were to follow Saint Laurent down any garden path you would find a pot of gold,"[5] – meaning that his designs would never disappoint.

THE END OF AN ERA
The stock market crash of 1987 was a wake-up call for the fashion industry and its insatiable consumers, and signaled the end of an era of ostentatious style. But it was the spread of the disease AIDS among the creative ranks of the fashion industry that brought a halt to the party. In the latter part of the decade, a host of design talent fell to the illnesses and infections that were associated with the virus that attacked the immune system, including Perry Ellis, Willi Smith, Angel Estrada, Patrick Kelly and Halston, to name a few. Investors began to think twice about backing male designers, and certainly the fashion business through the beginning of the 1990s felt the loss of these creators.

ABOVE A striking Yves Saint Laurent long dress, inspired by modern art, that appeared on the cover of *Life* magazine in 1966.

OPPOSITE For the autumn/winter 1976 *Ballets Russes* collection, a stunning gold lamé evening coat with jet embroidery by Lesage, by Yves Saint Laurent.

6 Back to the Future

Wearing distressed jeans and draped in Giorgio di Sant' Angelo T-shirts, framed against the Manhattan skyline, Naomi Campbell, Linda Evangelista, Tatjana Patitz, Christy Turlington and Cindy Crawford ushered in the new decade. Peter Lindbergh's January 1990 cover for British *Vogue* paid homage to the cover girls who had sold millions of dollars of luxury brands and had become known throughout the world as 'supermodels.' The black and white photograph presented them as natural beauties; leggy, glamorous, intelligent and every one a multi-millionaire.

The choice of clothes they wore in this photograph however, said more. It implied that however rich, famous or beautiful a woman you were, you no longer needed to flaunt it. The very nineties' concept of girl power had been established. So familiar and powerfully effective were they at selling a brand, they were referred to by their Christian names. They had become celebrities – modern-day stars in their own right.

Models were not the only women making waves during the 1990s. In politics record numbers of women were elected to high office in the US in 1992, the "Year of the Woman". Women reached the heights of power in the US government. Hilary Rodham Clinton led policy proposals, traveled abroad as a State

LEFT The faces that launched a thousand luxury brands; (L to R) Linda Evangelista, Cindy Crawford, Lauren Hutton, Beverley Johnson, Christy Turlington, and Naomi Campbell.

OPPOSITE The Spice Girls band at the Brit Awards in 1995. (L to R) Geri Halliwell, Victoria Adams, Emma Bunton, Melanie Brown and Melanie Chisholm.

Department representative to 82 nations, advised her husband, and was elected a Senator in 2000. Madeleine Albright and Janet Reno took two of the cabinet's top jobs as United States Secretary of State and United States Attorney General, respectively. The Spice Girls became one of the biggest global pop acts of the decade and Celine Dion became the best selling music artist of all time, with sales of over two hundred million albums and record numbers of women became top CEOs worldwide.

Kate Winslet wore Alexander McQueen's dress aptly named *titanic* to the Academy Awards ceremony in Los Angeles. The movie of the same name in which she starred took us back to a more romantic time in fashion and was a cultural phenomenon throughout the world, eventually it became the highest earning film of all time, grossing over $1.8 billion (£1.1 billion/€1.4 billion) worldwide.

There were many occasions to celebrate throughout the world: Peace in Northern Ireland with the Good Friday Agreement; the Warsaw Pact; the break-up of the Soviet Union on December 26, 1991; the release of African National Congress leader Nelson Mandela from jail in February 1990; and German reunification in 1990. After the fall of the Berlin Wall in November 1989, East and West Germany integrated their economic structure and provincial governments, focusing on the modernisation of the former communist East and spurring enormous growth in many of the world's most important economies.

After three decades of economic growth, Japan's economy crashed leading to what has been called the 'Lost Decade'. Advances in technology meant smaller mobile telephones and faster Internet connections. Portable CD players became very popular and had a profound impact on the music industry and youth culture during the 1990s. Apple introduced the iMac computer in 1998, initiating a trend in computer design towards translucent and multi-coloured cases.

THE FACES OF FASHION

Getting back to supermodels, in April 1992 it was American *Vogue's* turn to honour the whole team of supermodels on its cover to celebrate the magazine's 100th anniversary. Patrick Demarchelier placed one and all – Naomi Campbell, Cindy Crawford, Linda Evangelista, Yasmeen Ghauri, Elaine Irwin, Karen Mulder, Tatjana Patitz, Claudia Schiffer, Niki Taylor, and Christy Turlington at the top of the tree. They were on their best behaviour, all wearing Gap white shirts and jeans. It was also a fitting celebration of the end of an era.

Many new faces joined these golden girls during the next decade, notably Kate Moss. Waif-like and a mere five feet six inches tall, she was different from the others in every way. That quality, as well as her natural poise, beautiful heart-shaped face and ability to change her look as often as she did her clothes, has kept Moss in the limelight ever since. There were the perfect blondes such as Eva Herzigova and Nadja Auermann and a new breed of cool

RIGHT Newcomer, 'little' Kate Moss on the catwalk with Naomi Campbell and Christy Turlington for the 1993 Isaac Mizrahi show in New York.

Brits: Stella Tennant, Iris Palmer, Honor Fraser, Erin O'Connor and Karen Elson, all feted for their modern edge.

Madonna, who was all about girl power, certainly earned her status as the ultimate style icon of her generation, having carved out an image that changed as often as each record was released. But none gave as much of a kick than when she stepped out on stage during her 1990 *Blonde Ambition* tour in Jean Paul Gaultier's cone-bra corset. They shocked and thrilled the world with their innerwear as outerwear statement. She was glad to be his muse again in 1992 at a charity fashion show for amfAR, "dressed in black with her gold tooth as her only accessory," reported *Women's Wear Daily*. "At the end of the runway she paused to peel off a jacket, revealing one of Gaultier's harness dresses and a lot more." Mission accomplished!

THE SHAPES OF THE 90S

The 1990s were the dawning of a 'New Age' with an explosion of interest in ecology, mystical religion, crystals and healing; and the colour white blazed with an intensity that invigorated fashion. All-white collections were the way forward, a way of clearing the fashion palette; Rifat Ozbek's spring 1990 all-white line-up included embroidered biker jackets and tasseled skirts. Ozbek, a graduate of Central St. Martins, had picked up Designer of the Year Award at London's Fashion Week in 1989 and was enjoying his moment in fashion. Like the man

ABOVE Madonna steps out in one of Jean Paul Gaultier's 'harness' dresses at a charity show to benefit amfAR.

OPPOSITE Rifat Ozbek starts the new millennium in fresh monotone style. Yasmin Le Bon models a striking outfit of narrow stretch pants, blazer and camisole waistcoat.

himself, his clothes were always witty as well as being eminently wearable.

Fitted dresses were having a renaissance, replacing the hard-edged power suit and baggy shapes of the eighties. Diane von Furstenberg, the American designer who caused a sensation with her wrap dresses in the seventies, restarted her business in 1992 presenting a new line of dresses. Boldly printed and similar to the originals, bar a few tweaks here and there, she sold them for under $200 (£125/€160)at the time, igniting her business and propelling it into a global brand that continues to grow today.

Gianfranco Ferré, the exuberant Italian designer, had replaced Marc Bohan as creative director at Dior. Bohan moved to London in an attempt to resurrect the fading house of Norman Hartnell. Ferré was typically extravagant with his dimensions and colour palette for Dior, perhaps a little too much. Many designers offered shorts as an alternative to skirts, matched to jackets with more feminine styling. If daytime clothes concentrated on understatement, eveningwear still gloried in unbridled decoration.

Gianni Versace went from strength to strength. He dressed all the beautiful people with flamboyant style and now enjoyed the extra kudos of royal patronage. Princess Diana was an enthusiastic client who, after her divorce, never looked better than when she wore one of his figure-hugging sheath dresses. He was the master of show-stopping glamour and his company was clocking up a turnover of a cool billion dollars in the nineties.

Versace thought nothing of paying supermodel Christy Turlington $50,000 (£31,500/€40,000) to model exclusively in his show, knowing full well that he would be featured in every magazine and newspaper from Texas to Timbuktu. He realised early on that sex sells; and that if clothes make the woman, supermodels make the sales. Versace's trademark Medusa head was recognized and coveted worldwide.

Domenico Dolce and Stefano Gabbana established their brand Dolce & Gabbana in 1987, offering womanly lingerie looks with a Sicilian twist, transporting us to the worlds of Visconti and Antonioni, Sophia Loren and Monica Vitti. Their superb tailoring and show-stopping glamour attracted a long list of celebrity clients – Madonna famously wore their heavily jeweled bodysuit at the US premiere of her movie *In Bed with Madonna* and by the mid-nineties their annual turnover was more than $400 million (£250 million/€320 million). Their collections gradually became more eclectic and vaguely bohemian in the nineties. Hollywood celebrities still love their style, a look that can sometimes seem casually thrown together; but the secret of their success is that everything has always been underpinned in a manner similar to that of fifties couture.

OPPOSITE Gianfranco Ferré succeeded Marc Bohan at Dior but failed to wow – this cerise taffeta strapless dress with lace train is from the autumn/winter 1991/2 couture show.

LEFT Diana, Princess of Wales, never looked better than when she wore Versace; arriving at a benefit concert in Italy for Bosnian children in white Versace shift.

On the dress: ITALY D&G LOVE DOLCE & GABBANA ... ITALY ME BABY

LEFT Cindy Crawford gets away with wearing one of Dolce & Gabanna's more tongue-in-cheek creations made of printed and embroidered linen.

OPPOSITE The 'rock chick' look was a roaring success for Tom Ford at Gucci; shown at the Milan ready-to-wear for autumn/winter 1995.

GUCCI AND TOM FORD

By the 1990s, Italy's venerable Gucci Group was looking a bit tired. In 1989 Dawn Mello was hired away from Bergdorf Goodman to become Gucci's creative director; in 1990 she chose Tom Ford to join her, as head of the womenswear line. When Investcorp, who had already bought a 50% share in the Gucci family business, gained 100% control in 1993 they set about making the changes needed to revive the ailing brand. Mello left to return to New York, and Ford was named creative director of all Gucci products.

Born in Austin, Texas, Tom Ford grew up in Santa Fe, New Mexico, the son of real-estate agents. He studied architecture and art history before changing to fashion. He then worked for New York designers Cathy Hardwick and Perry Ellis before moving to Milan. There he met his long-time partner, Richard Buckley. Ford told *Newsweek* in March 1996: "Designing for a big company is like being a film director because you put so many elements together: The image, the windows, the ad campaign, the accessories. That's what interests me."[1]

Tom Ford became the golden boy of Florence at the Gucci Group in 1993 when he took over as creative director for the fabled but fumbling Italian accessories house and restored its lustre. His first retro-cool collection hit the right spot and had the show's models asking to be paid in silky lime-green shirts, velvet hip-huggers, shiny red stilettos – anything from the sexy modernist line would do. Ford had gone from being a relative unknown to flavour of the month and so began another fashion legend. Before long all of Hollywood was lining up for Ford's faux fur coats, patent leather go-go boots and chartreuse caftans.

There would be a frenzied rush at the Gucci stores for certain items each season. At the company's London store some 150 patient customers were wait-listed for his techno stretch pantsuit, and an amazing 300 for the men's leopard thong. In New York, Bergdorf Goodman had 220 hopefuls on hold for the silver and white leather pumps and the flagship store in Milan could not keep the best-selling G-belts in stock for more than a few hours. Other brands took note and an unparalleled escalation of luxury brand products followed.

Ford was a natural, not only as a creative force but also on the business side of fashion. He became the power behind one of Wall Street's hottest companies. Gucci's share price jumped from $22 to $42 and during his ten years at Gucci Group, sales increased from 230 million dollars in 1994 to almost 3 billion dollars in 2003, making Gucci one of the largest and most profitable luxury brands in the world.

The rapid growth and influence of LVMH, the first luxury goods conglomerate with a portfolio of more than 50 brands, including Louis Vuitton and Christian Dior, led to the emergence of a new sub-sector of luxury goods, and the growth of other conglomerates and corporate brands like the Gucci Group, Pinault Printemps Redoute, Richemont and the Prada Group.

In the mid-nineties investors went crazy over the prospect of initial public offerings from marquee fashion brands. Luxury firms were hotly pursued after big money was made on Gucci Group's IPO in October 1995. Investcorp,

LEFT One of Prada's best-selling bags in glossy red leather with signature triangular branding prominently displayed.

which owned all Gucci's stock, raised $1.4 billion (£880 million/€1.1 billion) from its sale of Gucci shares, a nifty profit after paying $246 million (£155 million/€197 million) for the company in the late 80s, before Tom Ford and Domenico De Sole engineered one of fashion's greatest comebacks. Many designers were made extremely wealthy after going public in the nineties including Ralph Lauren, Donna Karan, Calvin Klein and Tommy Hilfiger.

PRADA

Prada was the premier luggage maker for the Milanese elite when Miuccia Prada took control in the late seventies. Maria Bianchi Prada, known as Miuccia, had been the unlikely inheritor of the family luggage business founded by Miuccia's grandfather, Mario, in 1913. With no formal design background or sewing skills, Miuccia and her business manager, later to become her husband, Patrizio Bertelli, first extended the range by adding a few items of clothing such as T-shirts and scarves.

It was 1979 when Miuccia first released a set of backpacks and tote bags made out of tough military spec black nylon that her grandfather had used as coverings for steamer trunks. But they were not an immediate success. Throughout the eighties Prada developed the brand and their designs, including Prada's much sought after elegant shoes and sandals. It was not until 1983 that the series of black nylon handbags and backpacks, discreetly branded on the outside with a distinctive triangle of silver metal; became a hit. Prada became known worldwide. The firm's subtle branding appealed to the many wealthy and increasingly youthful customers who shopped in the boutiques. Miuccia's attitude to wealth, like much of the aristocracy, was that real power consists in concealing the fact that you have it.

By the nineties the partners had built Prada into an $800 million (£500 million/€640 million) business. A brand that enjoyed its position as a premium status symbol of the time, Prada had distinguished itself as being a place to find unconventional clothes cut in unique shapes, with an interesting use of pattern and the newest technical fabrics. They launched Prada womenswear and menswear lines, and a less expensive collection called Miu Miu, (her nickname) inspired by Muiccia's personal wardrobe. In 1998 they launched Prada Sport, their high-tech line of sports-inspired shoes and clothing.

By 1999 Bertelli had acquired Jil Sander. He also negotiated joint ventures with Helmut Lang, but neither acquisition worked out as planned. The company also acquired Italian eyewear maker De Rigo and a stake in the British footwear company Church & Co.

LEFT Miuccia Prada is a success at the 1993 Bryant Park, New York collections.

Miuccia Prada's open distaste for the increasingly constricting dictates of fashion, combined with a willingness to experiment, have continued to bewitch fashion insiders. Her love of quirky vintage periods mixes with ideas drawn from her own style. She never throws anything away and keeps her clothes in a separate apartment. Today the Prada Group is a privately owned luxury goods conglomerate and continues to enjoy a prominent place in the global fashion market.

LOOKING FORWARD

Looking back, much of the nineties seemed to be about referencing the fifties, sixties and seventies; but London's art colleges were producing new talent such as the forward-looking Alexander McQueen, Stella McCartney, and the fashion artist, Hussein Chalayan. Chalayan first attracted attention by burying his debut collection underground "to achieve the right texture of the fabric," and made stylish suits from paper, wood and even chair covers. His shows became intriguing and not-to-be-missed installations.

In 1993 Alexander McQueen set up his own design studio in London. He had spent time as an apprentice to Savile Row tailors, as well as working with a theatrical costumier; and worked with the brilliant but little known London-based Japanese designer Koji Tatsuno before going to Milan to work with Romeo Gigli.

RIGHT Kate Moss wears a vintage, almost 'granny' look of mis-matched pattered tweed suit at the Prada spring/summer 1996 collection in Milan.

Returning to London, he completed an M.A. at Central St. Martins School of Art where his final collection caught the attention of *Vogue* editor Isabella Blow, who bought the entire collection, much like Joan Burstein had done when John Galliano graduated from Central St. Martin's a few years before. With this endorsement, Lee McQueen's reputation was soon established and his road to success ensured. In 1996 at the age of 27, McQueen became one of the youngest to achieve the title British Fashion Designer of the Year.

VIVIENNE WESTWOOD'S 90S COLLECTIONS

Vivienne Westwood was awarded British Designer of the Year in 1990 and 1991. She became academically accepted in 1992 when awarded an Honorary Senior Fellow of the Royal College of Art and the same year received an O.B.E. from the Queen. No wonder she continued throughout the nineties with her Anglophile collections, the British Empire and its uniforms forming the basis of her inspiration, along with her fascination with

BELOW Linda Evangelista wears a sweeping emerald green taffeta ball gown at Vivienne Westwood's Paris couture show for spring/summer 1996.

the interchange of fashion influence between England and France.

Each collection became a 'history of costume' lesson with Vivienne. For autumn/winter 1990 she used photographic printing of Old Master paintings on silk and wool combined with as many different quantities of fabric as possible, creating a feeling of richness. For the following spring collection which she named *Cut, Slash and Pull,* she lowered hemlines to an elegant lower calf, using slashed and frayed fabrics, and created giant circular shapes treated as Greek chiton. Later collections included *Dressing Up,* a culmination of past collections; and *Salon,* influenced by 20th century couture, particularly Christian Dior. *Always on Camera* was a parody of French couture, mixed with the imagery of Hollywood icons such as Marlene Dietrich, and photographically printed on denim.

Westwood was on a roll with the *Grand Hotel* collection where fifties cuts were exaggerated, accessorized with ten inch heels, in which Naomi Campbell famously tripped and fell from the runway in Paris. *Anglomania* describes the French passion at the end of the 1800s for all things English, as did *Café Society, On Liberty* and *Erotic Zones.* All manner of coquettishness followed with *Vive la Cocotte,* in winter 1995, and *Les Femmes* in 1996.

GRUNGE

'Grunge' fashion appeared to be the ugly side of early nineties trends. With its origins in the Seattle-based music scene of the same name, particularly the grunge band, Nirvana, it was

read as a reaction to the excesses of the eighties, and what began as a counterculture fashion soon spread to the mainstream. It was a style of dressing down. Clothing items looked worn, were either too large or too small, and were frequently purchased from thrift shops.

Its followers wore layers of clothes – flannel shirts, shorts and long johns, Doc Martens, matted hair and knitted hats. Vintage frocks were roughed up with heavy boots and make-up was off the menu. Marc Jacobs, who had just been promoted to creative designer at the US fashion house, Perry Ellis, was immediately impressed and in 1992 designed a whole collection around the idea. But his thrift-store staples reinterpreted in luxury fabrics, the cashmere long johns, checked shirts made of washed silk, heavy army-style boots and crocheted skull caps worn over lank hair did not sell. *Women's Wear Daily* hailed Jacobs as the "guru of grunge". But nobody wanted to pay high prices for thrift-shop chic and it cost him his job. Nevertheless, grunge in its many different forms influenced High Street fashion for many a season.

Calvin Klein saw a way to exploit the idea further by using the waif-like image of the young Kate Moss for his 1997 advertisements. This ultimately backfired on the company because of a simultaneous trend on the edge of fashion coined 'heroin chic': a look characterized by pale skin, dark circles under the eyes, and, worse, jutting bones – an extreme expression of early nineties economic recession. The look promoted emaciated features and androgyny that stood in direct opposition to the healthy

LEFT Model, Yasmin Le
Bon poses backstage
before the ill-fated Perry
Ellis spring/summer
1993 grunge collection
designed by Marc Jacobs

OPPOSITE Alexander
McQueen's infamous
'bumpster' trouser design
from the spring/summer
1994 collection in
London, starting a trend for
low-slung jeans.

and vibrant looks of previous role models such as Cindy Crawford, Claudia Schiffer, and Heidi Klum.

Heroin had infiltrated pop culture through attention brought to addictions in the early 1990s.[2] The heroin chic trend coincided with a string of movies such as *Trainspotting* and *Pulp Fiction* that were criticized for glamorising heroin. There were also those who defended the look. Jacob Sullem of *Reason* magazine said, "There is no reason to expect that people attracted to the look promoted by Calvin Klein and other advertisers…will also be attracted to heroin, any more than suburban teenagers who wear baggy pants and backward caps will end up shooting people from moving cars."[3] The advertisements were, however, withdrawn when US President Bill Clinton stepped in and strongly supported the anti-drug groups.

HIP-HOP

Hip-hop was another sub-cultural music-inspired fashion trend with a unique style that included baggy pants, tracksuits and bold gold jewellery, or 'bling.' Karl Lagerfeld was the first to bring the look to the runway in 1991 with his *Nouveau Rapper* collection for Chanel, complete with quilted leather jackets, baseball caps worn backwards and plenty of bling – gold nameplates and chain jewellery. Isaac Mizrahi, the darling of New York fashion in the 90s, also did a witty take on the trend, accessorising his collection with oversized gold Star of David medallions. Even Alexander McQueen's notorious 'bumster' trousers reflected hip-hop sensibilities.

While the original roots of hip-hop were based in African and African American music, the hip-hop that arose in the 1970s began in New York City. The B-boys (break boys) of the 1970s (their female followers were called flygirls) developed an athletic dance style. This led to a new feel good, feel-fit cool look and a move towards a more relaxed dress code. Now everyone was limbering up in sports-inspired clothing: Prada's hooded gabardine sweatshirts, Helmut Lang's techno fabrics, Velcro fastenings at Jil Sander and skateboarding-inspired zip-front cardigans from Marc Jacobs. Certain brands of sneakers, sports shoes and bags hit an all time high, so much so that luxury labels such as Prada opened special departments for them and the Nike brand achieved almost-couture status.

THE MINIMALISTS: JIL SANDER AND HELMUT LANG

Jil Sander was a prominent minimalist working from her Munich base in the nineties. Having established her company in Germany, Sander debuted in Paris in 1993. Her designs exemplified the great skill required to produce beautiful clothing without the use of embellishment to create interest. She favoured simple lines and displayed architectural considerations, using luxurious fabrics. Minimalist style was just as expensive as the

RIGHT Helmut Lang embraced American sportswear. His model wears a silver padded jacket and pant at the autumn 1999 collection in New York.

OPPOSITE A wide-leg jumpsuit with matching jacket in brown linen from the spring/summer 1992 collection of the elegant minimalist designer, Jil Sander.

ostentatious look of a few years earlier but that did not deter Sander's clients. Her cool collections were highly sought after throughout the decade and left an indelible impression; like Calvin Klein before her she was perfectly in tune with the mood for understated style.

Helmut Lang became a major architect of early nineties minimalism with his skinny trouser suits, tight metallic T-shirts and dark denim jeans. Up until 1996 Lang had been based in Austria and would show in Paris at the usual bi-annual timings of the ready-to-wear, but having visited New York, he fell in love with the city and moved his business there. In July 1998, he announced his intention to show his spring/ summer collection in New York in September, before the scheduled fashion week, with an astonishing effect. Within days, Calvin Klein and Donna Karan declared they'd show that week too, setting in motion a breakaway group of New York shows scheduled to go before London, Milan and Paris.

The 42-year-old Lang had kept a low profile for ten years, operating his business quietly, based in Vienna, from where he delivered a convincingly wearable, loved and relied-upon urban uniform for a global audience of men and women. For his New York debut he produced a sublime collection of luxurious parkas, warm, light and totally functional topcoats of down and alpaca to layer over ribbed cashmere sweaters, ivory moleskin jeans and cargo pants. There

RIGHT A classic, skinny trouser suit and white shirt designed by Helmut Lang from the autumn/winter 1999 collection.

were the signature black suits, simply perfect v-necks and fabulous dark denim.

Lang's aesthetic defined the shifting 1990s as succinctly as Armani's did in the 1980s and Yves Saint Laurent's did in the 1970s. Lang told Mark Holgate of American *Vogue* in 2010 that "One of the biggest achievements in Paris is to be called a *createur*, which means the French regard you as an artist in your field, while in New York, recognition is manifested through glamour, commercial credibility, your potential as a brand."[4]

Just as Lang's move to New York had been accepted by the fashion flock, he decided to stop staging runway shows altogether, and threw fashion editors into complete uproar by posting his autumn/winter 1998 collection on the Internet. He told Sarah Mower in *Harper's Bazaar*, "I felt the whole focus of what we were doing was building up to a major event, and suddenly it was an issue for me. I'd been thinking about using the Internet for a long time, so it just seemed the moment to do it. It also felt right to keep contact with Europe, because it was the first season we didn't do a show in Paris. We could be global; everyone could see the clothes at the same time. It's democratic. You know – modern communication."[5]

This courageous designer never attended fashion school, never assisted a designer, and never wooed the press to gain attention. He drew inspiration from his background in

Austria, the beat of techno music, the clothes he remembered wearing as a child, the dark, single breasted suits of Balkan emigrants, and the vests and anoraks that he wore for sports as a schoolboy, translating them into clothes that earned him a reputation for not only being avant-garde, but also creating on his own terms. In 2005 however, Lang decided to sell his company to become an artist. Now based in the US, he has never returned to Vienna. His projects have included fashion-related subjects such as shredding part of his 6,000-piece archive, which were turned into sculptures; and an installation called *Front Row* consisting of a cast row of simple folding white chairs, like the ones he used at shows in Paris, exhibited in 2009 at the Museum of Modern Art in Frankfurt.[6]

EXPERIMENTS IN FASHION

Deconstruction of clothes was another popular way of redefining fashion in the nineties, rejecting all the customary rules and breaking all conventions. The trend was started by the Japanese avant-gardists Rei Kawakuba and Yohji Yamamoto, who had introduced themselves to Paris and the world in the eighties. They showed inside-out seams, pockets askew, frayed hems and linings on the outside, along with oversized proportions such as long arms. It was a general taking-apart and putting back together of familiar pieces in unexpected ways

and placements. Designers who were once just unpronounceable names in the 80s – Martin Margiela, Ann Demeulemeester and Dries Van Noten – became familiar as their deconstructed looks were snapped up.

Issey Miyake's late-eighties experiment with pleating, in order to develop more flexibility in movement, evolved into the launch of the highly innovative and successful *Pleats Please* collection in 1993. The process used involved cutting and sewing the garments first, then placing them between layers of paper to be fed through a heated press for pleating. Miyake's basic tenets for making clothes has always been the idea of creating a garment from one piece of cloth; and the exploration of the space between the body and the cloth that covers it. His approach to design was to strike a consistent balance between tradition and innovation, handicrafts and new technology. *Pleats Please* was a radical, eminently practical, and universal form of contemporary clothing that combined all these components in one beautiful idea. Lightweight and washable, they have won the respect and admiration of women throughout the world.

Hussein Chalayan began to establish a reputation that dispelled the theory that fashions only relationship to fine art is a derivative one. Still independent, he is a progressive designer who does his own thing and has many celebrity followers for his streamlined clothes,

OPPOSITE Dries Van Noten's eclectic style consistently delights his clients. A black lace evening ensemble with embroidered mid-calf length skirt from the summer 2000 collection.

LEFT Contemporary, textural and with a positive attitude, there is an austere beauty to Belgian designer Anne Demeulemeester's designs.

including the actress Tilda Swinton. Chalayan's work recently attracted new attention in a retrospective exhibition called *Narratives* at the Musée des Arts Décoratifs in Paris during the latter part of 2011. The exhibition featured about 70 garments dating from Hussein's 1993 Central St Martins College graduate collection through to his autumn/winter 2011 collection.

Over the two floors Chalayan showed a body of work that makes it hard to define whether he is a fashion designer or an artist.

LUXURY RETURNS

Perestroika and the fall of the Berlin Wall in 1989 had liberated the Soviet bloc, converting it into a capitalist society with an insatiable appetite for western goods and services, the more luxurious the better. A flood of new models from Eastern Europe paraded the international runways, some became well known, others celebrities in their own right, such as the exceptionally beautiful young Russian model Natalia Vodianova.

In 1991 Pierre Bergé at Yves Saint Laurent declared to *Women's Wear Daily,* "Haute couture is dead." But the moneymen were determined to keep couture brands alive by expanding their product portfolios and placing increased emphasis on accessories like leather goods, sunglasses and jewellery, responding to consumer demand from new markets in Eastern Europe and Asia.

By the mid-nineties the economy was looking up, the stock market had climbed and Wall Street analysts were not far off when they attributed the stock market's incredible surges to "irrational exuberance." This term applied to fashion in the nineties as well. Luxury brands expanded as if there were no tomorrow. Financial independence among a large number of young working women with an educated eye for fashion was leading designers to a different place in the nineties.

Women who had held back on high fashion indulgences were now looking for ways of rewarding themselves, simply because they

OPPOSITE More of an installation than a fashion show, Hussein Chalayan's presentation at the Sadler's Wells Theatre showed models in shift dresses put on hair covers, the last stepping inside a table that opened out into a wooden skirt.

ABOVE Sculpted dress that looks like pink candy floss from artist/designer Hussein Chalayan's 1999 collection.

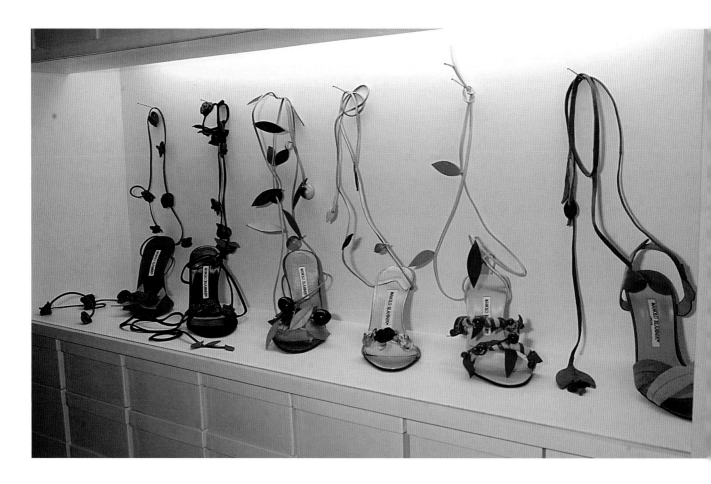

were worth it. First it was shoes - Prada, Gucci, Ferragamo or Manolo. Then it was handbags - Chanel, Gucci, Hermès, Louis Vuitton and Fendi were the most desired. Now they could afford the big-ticket items independently young professionals began to set their sights on long-lasting quality items such as watches – nothing pretentious, a Cartier or Rolex would do, or maybe a Tiffany pearl necklace, discreet and elegant under her sleek grey trouser suit by Helmut Lang.

On the West Coast of America Hollywood's favourite, the Fred Segal store, had been which

established as the place to go for something that little bit different since the 1960s, had now evolved into one of the first 'destination' fashion stores. Back then, with its glorious vines that covered the white walls of the ever-chic store at the corner of Melrose Avenue and Crescent Heights Boulevard, it was inspirational. The store included restaurants where you could see and be seen by Hollywood's finest. So familiar was it to stylish Americans that in the 1995 movie *Clueless*, Alicia Silverstone who played Cher, the designer mall rat with a heart as big as her dad's bank account, asks her maid when trying to put an outfit together for her drivers license, "Lucy! Where's my white collarless shirt from Fred Segal?!"

Similar stores began to open all over the world, most notably 10 Corso Como in Milan that opened in 1991 in a converted garage and Colette, the three floor, 8,000 square feet concept store on the prestige Rue St. Honoré in Paris where you can not only shop for hip fashion, but also buy a coffee table book or music CD, have a meal, try more than one hundrerd different kinds of water in the water bar or view an exhibition in their spacious galleries. It was and so remains an enjoyable shopping experience under one stylish roof.

Luxurious and architecturally inspired store designs created a selling atmosphere to enhance brand image. Technical innovations developed that enhanced sales such as advanced information technology for inventory management, and for controlling and tracking product stock and delivery. Technology also provided a new channel of retail and distribution through the Internet. But the dot.com crash of the late 1990s, typified by the failure of the first e-retail start-up company, boo.com, discouraged the adoption of Internet retailing

during this decade. The Internet, however, increased the influence of celebrities on fashion trends, as well as speeding up the global proliferation of trends.

HIGH-END CALIFORNIA CASUAL

A new kind of glamour emerged from the West Coast of America around this time. Young, tanned and fit Californian girls were ready for expensive brands such as Juicy Couture, Bisou Bisou and BCBG. Gela Nash and Pamela Skaist-Levy started Juicy Couture in 1997 with the aim of producing athletic and casually styled girly clothes and slogan T- shirts with a glamorous twist. Their unique selling proposition was that nothing would cost under one hundred dollars. Their luxurious velour tracksuits in candy-coloured pastels were embroidered with the

Juicy Couture name in gold and soon became every Hollywood actress's essential for Rodeo Drive shopping trips. And when Madonna started to wear Juicy Couture, personalised with "Madge" embroidery, the company became an instant success.

Parisian Michele Bohbot brought a large measure of French chic to California when she launched her fashion company Bisou Bisou (French for "a little kiss") in 1989. Her sportswear, denim and one-of-a-kind dresses along with all the trimmings – shoes, handbags and costume jewellery – were also met with immediate success and today are sold under license by the mighty J.C. Penney.

BCBG stands for Bon Chic Bon Genre, which means, "good style good attitude" in French. It is a brand started by French Tunisian

Max Azria and his wife Lubova. They moved to California from Paris in 1981 when they opened a boutique call Jess. In 1989 he founded BCBG, it was a new 'concept' store offering hip French clothing. Again, chic French style had captured the hearts of Hollywood A-listers, and the husband and wife team began designing clothes for TV shows such as *Friends*, *Seinfeld*, and *Entertainment Tonight*. They also dressed celebrity customers such as Sharon Stone, Uma Thurman and Madonna. In 1999 BCBG bought out the Paris house of Hervé Léger, famous for the sexy, body-hugging banded dresses. Today they remain a high profile brand in Hollywood and the rest of the world.

FASHION FOR THE MASSES

At the same time, mass market fashion had a direct impact on the luxury fashion sector in the nineties. Mass fashion grew rapidly as a result of advanced and cheaper manufacturing, better design and more dynamic retail techniques. Fast fashion brands like Zara from Spain, H&M from Sweden and Top Shop from Britain began to produce high fashion style at low cost, offering consumers luxury fashion alternatives at significantly lower prices – and in quick succession to their appearance on the catwalks. Consumers were becoming more demanding and assertive. To keep up and ensure their brand name remained prominent, top designers such as Armani, Yves Saint Laurent, Christian Lacroix and Versace launched lower priced ranges and stand-alone stores such as Armani's A/X, YSL Variations, Bazaar and Versus.

With the fashion business becoming more corporate, change was taking place in the hallowed halls of the couture. The couture had been in the hands of an older generation of more established designers, set in their ways, and had taken on a curiously quaint aura. Elegance on the whole was found more often in vintage than in the salons of couture houses, and many of them were at risk of closure. Even the noble Jacques Mouclier, honorary president of the Chambre Syndicale, realised the need to revitalise Paris couture and in 1996 made the radical move of opening up the couture ranks, which had already dwindled to 15 couturiers, to ready-to-wear designers. Thierry Mugler and Jean Paul Gaultier were the first to participate.

BRITISH DESIGNERS TAKE OVER FRENCH COUTURE

After 43 years Hubert de Givenchy retired with the elegance you would expect from an old-school couturier. Graciously he dedicated his last winter 1995 haute couture collection to the heads of his ateliers. Although it was sad to see yet another legendary figure disappear, life, fashion and technology were changing at a frightening speed.

In 1996 John Galliano was chosen to succeed the aristocratic Givenchy, making history as the first British designer to head a French couture house since Charles Frederick Worth. The man who looked like a pirate with his hoop earring, knickerbockers and matinee idol moustache, whose designs were just as swashbuckling as his shows were spectacular, was to become heir to Hubert de Givenchy, the man who dressed Audrey Hepburn to

ABOVE In 1996 John Galliano entered the hallowed salons of Paris haute couture as the first British couturier to become creative director at Givenchy.

OPPOSITE By 1997 John Galliano had moved to the top job at Christian Dior and began refreshing the Christian Dior ready-to-wear line as well as the couture; gold brocade evening dress is from the Dior ready-to-wear line.

perfection in *Breakfast at Tiffany's* and helped Jackie Kennedy and Princess Grace to become the epitome of global fashions. Givenchy believed Galliano's youth and outrageousness would make a fashion statement loud enough to be heard in the stores of Shanghai and Tokyo.

Chairman Bernard Arnault, whose luxury goods conglomerate LVMH included Givenchy, Dior, Louis Vuitton and Loewe, was determined to inject new life and fresh excitement into his

brands; and this controversial appointment was just the start. Two years later Galliano was offered the top couture prize: Arnault moved him to Dior as creative director, replacing Galliano at Givenchy with another edgy Brit, the arrogant and hugely talented Alexander McQueen, whose London collections and highly theatrical shows had also impressed LVMH. When questioned by the French media about his choice of British designers, Arnault

ABOVE Stella McCartney gets a little help from her friends at the debut of her design directorship at Paris fashion house Chloé at the spring/summer 1998 collection.

explained that England was the country currently producing the finest talent.

Stella McCartney, not long graduated from Central St. Martins, was trained on Savile Row and apprenticed to Christian Lacroix. McCartney's was the third surprise appointment to a French house when, at the age of 25, she was made creative director at Chloé in 1997. Her first collection combined lacy petticoat skirts with fine tailoring and was hailed a triumph. McCartney continues to refine her style and expand under her own name brand with increasing success today.

The mid-nineties saw a return to ladylike dressing. There was a feeling that haute couture no longer had to compete with the ready-to-wear which was reflected with new opulence. Some couture designers dispensed altogether with day wear, instead concentrating on fabulous evening fantasies. Others, such as Karl Lagerfeld for Chanel, displayed such refinements as a coat made from organza that graduated to a hemline embroidered as if by magic with feathers that could only be achieved by the *petit mans* of a couture house.

Once started, there seemed no stopping of designer imports to the European houses. American Michael Kors went to Celine, and New Jersey-born Narciso Rodriguez to Spanish design house Loewe. Rodriquez was virtually unknown until 1996 when he designed Carolyn Bessette Kennedy's bias-cut satin wedding dress. Alber Elbaz, who had worked with Geoffrey Beene, went to Guy Laroche and Marc Jacobs moved to Louis Vuitton.

LEFT Mixed print trouser suit from the ill-fated 1993 Perry Ellis *Grunge* collection. Marc Jacobs's ideas have since proved to be ahead of his time.

MARC JACOBS

New Yorker Marc Jacobs' grandmother taught him to knit as a child and at age 15 he worked as a stock boy in New York's then hot new store Charivari, where he was introduced to Perry Ellis. Ellis's cool attitudes to fashion and obvious success inspired Jacobs to study fashion. At Parsons School of Art and Design he became a star pupil, winning the Perry Ellis Golden Thimble Award in 1984, and in the same year the Chester Weinberg Gold Thimble Award and the Design Student of the Year Award. Two years later he launched his own business with best friend, Robert Duffy, as creative collaborator and business partner. They formed Jacobs Duffy Designs Inc., which continues to this day.

In 1986, with backing from the Japanese company Onward Kashiyama USA, Inc., Jacobs designed his first collection bearing his own name. Jacobs became the youngest designer to have ever been awarded the fashion industry's highest tribute, the Council of Fashion Designers of America's Perry Ellis Award for New Fashion Talent. In 1988, Jacobs and Duffy joined the women's design studio of Perry Ellis after its founder had died, as president and vice president, respectively. Continuing his successful and still short career, in 1992 the Council of Fashion Designers of America awarded Jacobs with the most prestigious Women's Designer of the Year Award. This also happened to be the year Jacobs launched his ill-fated *Grunge* collection, leading to his dismissal from the company.

Marc Jacobs has always been the darling of his models who often, in the early days, worked for him for free. His immense charm and wit has consistently translated into pretty, optimistic collections and since Jacobs was appointed Louis Vuitton's creative director in 1997, he has done no wrong, consistently triumphing with admired and newsworthy ready-to-wear collections as well as applying his ideas and whimsical style to the ever important Louis Vuitton accessories. His own labels, Marc Jacobs and the secondary line, Marc by Marc Jacobs, continue to thrive and expand. Jacobs is now based in Paris where he is known as an enthusiastic collector of contemporary art as well as a respected fashion designer.

A YEAR OF EXTREMES

Nineteen ninety-seven was a year of wild extremes as consumers tracked the giddy heights of the stock exchange and then were crushed by the tragic loss of Gianni Versace and Princess Diana. Britain's New Labour government, led by the smooth-talking Tony Blair promised a better future for all and a great opportunity to promote 'Cool Britannia' and the country's richly creative design force as its best asset. Hong Kong was handed back to the Chinese and there followed a passion for Chinoiserie. Heels became stiletto high or clumpy Chinese clogs. Rei Kawakubo stuffed her clothes with pillows to hunchback proportions, claiming that she was reinventing the body.

Alexander McQueen and John Galliano had put London back on the fashion map. Galliano garnered rave reviews for his debut collection at Dior, while there was less enthusiasm for McQueen at Givenchy. McQueen stayed with the house until March 2001, continuing to create challenging collections, including one featuring car robots spraying paint over white cotton dresses, and double amputee model Aimee Mullins striding down the catwalk on intricately carved wooden legs; until the contract that was "constraining his creativity" was ended.

JOHN GALLIANO AT DIOR

Bernard Arnault's decision to move John Galliano from Givenchy to Dior meant all eyes were focused on the man who would, like the original founder of the house, bring excitement back into the couture. Galliano's appointment also happened to mark the 50th anniversary of Christian Dior's first and most influential collection, the 1947 New Look. For his house debut Galliano revisited the Belle Époque period, but with a 21st century kick, though his respect for Dior was evident throughout the collection.

Galliano's Belle Époque models donned skinny suits and notice-me Masai jewellery. Jackets had exaggerated collars, peplums, and drapes. The designer chose lightweight black and white tweed, a Christian Dior favourite. Galliano's version was closely-cut on the curve, shown with micro-mini and floor-length skirts. For the cocktail hour each outfit was stunning, the corseted bodices cut from patterned silks inspired by Egypt and English flower gardens. Each dress was chosen to suit the model wearing it – a black tulle dress heavy with jet embroidery for Carla Bruni, a yellow silk sheath for Claudia Schiffer.

Arnault's gamble on Galliano had paid off. "The day after the collection the salons were packed with private clients. Appointments were scheduled solidly from 8.30a.m to 7.30p.m. The three couture salons were filled to capacity and the directrice de couture, Caroline Grouvelle, was forced to conduct fittings in her office,"[7] Women's Wear Daily wrote on January 22, 1997. As sometimes happens, all the haute couture houses were in harmony the winter of 1997 with a return to the Belle Èpoque, featuring sumptuous laces and silks, all adorned with masses of glistening jet.

Haute couture was hot again, thanks to the electrifying influence of a new generation of couturiers. John Galliano, Jean Paul Gaultier and Alexander McQueen proved that transgression was cool. Exhibitionism was the operative word, pure fin de siècle fantasy, boosted by the unexpected presence of Hollywood celebrities. It seemed every star worth an award wanted to wear a couture frock and jewels to match. Madonna had started a trend following her starring role in Evita of treating every movie premiere like Oscar night, turning up at each one dressed in a different outfit. No one understands the significance of a drop-dead entrance more than Hollywood, and when Nicole Kidman wore a chinoiserie-inspired dress by Galliano to the Oscars in March 1997 she appeared on front pages worldwide, further endorsing the glamour of couture.

THE END OF THE MILLENIUM

US Vogue celebrated the end of the century with a Millennium Special. The cover, photographed by Annie Leibovitz, extended threefold to include three generations of fashion models; a compendium of the faces that had inspired and launched thousands of fashion trends. Amongst them were the beautiful veterans such as Lauren Hutton and Iman, Paulina Porizkova, Stephanie

Seymour and Patti Hansen; along with the
supers and new girls, such as Kate Moss
and the tall, sexy Brazilian superstar, Gisele
Bündchen.

Back on the runway women were portrayed
as strong and powerful, and occasionally as
angry, tough and aggressive. Although this
image was not new for ready-to-wear, it was
unknown in couture. Alexander McQueen's
second couture collection for Givenchy in

1997 was held at a medical school on
the outskirts of Paris and titled *Elect Dissect*.
The idea, a little dark but logical enough,
showcased McQueen as a kind of Dr.
Frankenstein who cuts up various historical,
ethnic and cultural styles and stitches them
back together into something new.

The decade that had seen minimalism,
materialism, and mass-market fashion moved,
a bit uncertainly, into a new millennium.

7 A Fashion Democracy

The financial power of the fashion conglomerates gathered speed at the beginning of the new millennium. In January 2000, the Gucci Group acquired Yves Saint Laurent and YSL Beauté and were looking for new designers. Alexander McQueen was poached from Givenchy and set up his own label under the group's umbrella, and in 2001 Stella McCartney left Chloé to join the Gucci fold.

OPPOSITE In cool, graphic white a dramatic floor-length dress with embroidered bodice and flower-ruffled skirt, by Sarah Burton for Alexander McQueen, autumn/winter 2011.

RIGHT A delicate black and white pinafore bodice evening dress by Stefano Pilati at Yves Saint Laurent for spring/summer 2004 ready-to-wear show in Paris.

Tom Ford assumed the position of creative director of Yves Saint Laurent and YSL Beauté, making Alber Elbaz, who was designing the ready-to-wear, redundant. In July 2002 Pinault Printemps Redoute, which had purchased the remaining Gucci shares from LVMH, made Ford vice-chairman of the management board of Gucci Group; but in April 2004 he resigned from his post following the failure of contract negotiations.

A year later Ford formed his own brand that continues today to perform and impress with his irresistible form of Hollywood glamour. Stefano Pilati, whose aim was to make the Saint Laurent brand "much more French" followed in Tom Ford's giant footsteps as creative director for YSL. His debut drew on the 1967 film *Belle de Jour*, in which the double life of its prostitute heroine, Séverine, was played by long-time YSL muse, Catherine Deneuve.

In 2000 Julien Macdonald was appointed successor to Alexander McQueen as chief designer at the Paris house of Givenchy, and in 2001, he was named British Fashion Designer of the Year. Born in Merthyr Tydfil, Macdonald was taught knitting by his mother. When he left the Royal College of Art with an MA, he went to work with Karl Lagerfeld at Chanel as head designer of knitwear between 1996 and 1998. His collections were sexy, glamorous and much loved by celebrities. Macdonald left Paris in 2004 to concentrate on his eponymous label and is now based in London's Mayfair and manufactures in Italy.

The September 11, 2001 terrorist attacks on the World Trade Center's twin towers in New York happened on the third day of the New York fashion collections, casting a dark shadow on events for the rest of the year. Like millions of others in the world, the fashion community

struggled to find anything definitive to say in the aftermath of the attacks, which not only damaged the economic picture, but changed global politics and society in many ways.

On television, thanks to Sarah Jessica Parker who starred in the hit sitcom *Sex and the City* (1998 – 2004) as Carrie Bradshaw, a fictional New York newspaper columnist dedicated to fashion with a massive footwear fetish, shoe designers such as Jimmy Choo, Manolo Blahnik and Christian Louboutin were catapulted into the limelight. The character of Carrie Bradshaw had a massive influence on the name recognition of luxury brand designers she admired and wore in the series, confessing "she would rather buy *Vogue* than dinner" and describing a Louis Vuitton bag as "the best money I ever spent." Net-a-porter sold out of the Vivienne Westwood wedding dress Carrie wore in the first movie version of the series.

Patricia Field was the series' costume designer whose styling was influential and used a mix of designer and vintage looks, and although the series was not written to promote fashion, it became symbolic of the decade's fascination with fashion, designers and luxury.

The successes and tragedies of the two British designers, John Galliano and Alexander McQueen, were also played out in the press, feeding the public's fascination for fashion during the first years of the new millennium with their mix of unbridled creativity and the dark side of genius.

GALLIANO IN THE SPOTLIGHT

Never really out of the spotlight since his appointment as creative director at Dior, the young punk John Galliano lived up to his reputation by presenting one of the most controversial haute couture fashion shows ever staged: Hobo chic was the theme for spring 2000, inspired by the homeless people Galliano observed while out jogging along the Seine. His chiffon-clad tramps wore dresses deconstructed into exquisite dishabille, layered over newsprint skirts, as if to keep them warm. Makeshift jewellery included strings of assorted garbage from broken kitchen utensils to dented tin cans and miniature whisky bottles. Galliano's creative audacity, his unbounded imagination and obvious affection for the down and outs was not applauded. The reaction was universal, from fashion critics to social welfare societies: they were appalled.

After such obvious rejection, Galliano made a public apology saying, "I never wanted to make a spectacle of misery," and carried on fantasising and making lots of money for his employers, LVMH. The name Dior was never out of the news, and the accessories, ready-to-wear, perfumes and menswear were all a roaring success.

Galliano became famous for his fashion presentations that were more like extravagant theatrical performances, months in the making. Galliano's research trips were legendary – to Turkey, India, Japan, Tibet, Egypt. He would take an entourage to collect artefacts and mementos that became essential components in his multifarious, romantic quest for the exquisite. One member of Galliano's team at Dior told Colin McDowell that John was like a method actor who "doesn't just design the collection - he becomes the collection."[1]

Arnault gave Galliano carte blanche to produce ever more extravagant, expansive shows, so it was not surprising that after the autumn/winter 2005 collection inspired by Teddy Boys, with exaggerated make-up (a Galliano/Dior constant) and Elvis flares, Suzy Menkes of *The New York Times* called on Galliano "to project Dior into the modern world again."

Bernard Arnault could not ignore Menkes' words or risk the billions of dollars that bad publicity could cost the company. Dior's ready-to-wear became markedly more conventional and with his 2007 'back to basics' collection Galliano was seen to be severely reined-back, his wings clipped by the company's focus on share prices and market growth. The collection was not judged to be a success.

The same year Galliano's right-hand man, Steven Robinson, died of cardiac arrest at the age of 38. He had worked by Galliano's side since 1988 when he was a 17-year-old intern. Friends would say that Stephen was very nurturing and looked after John. Robinson also acted as a link to the outside world. However, the glories of Galliano's couture lived on and after the dazzling effort for spring 2007 that melded geisha exotica with New Look chic, *Women's Wear Daily* wrote, "Galliano has put couture back on its high-fashion pedestal."

OPPOSITE John Galliano's 'Hobo' look presented on the Paris catwalk for spring/summer 2000 did not go down well with the Christian Dior clients or the press.

RIGHT Galliano featured giant collars on oversized coats and massive bows as an exaggeration of the founder's style and Geisha-influenced make-up for Dior's autumn/winter 2004 collection.

Dior bought a majority stake in Galliano's own label in 2008, putting more pressure on the designer to make a profit. Galliano admitted to suffering panic attacks as he took on more licences "in order for the house of Galliano to survive". Menswear, womenswear, children's clothing, perfume, jewellery, shoes, beachwear…the work increased very fast and as the pressure mounted Galliano battled with the competing demands of Dior and Galliano. Galliano's schedule was crippling, but for a designer of his capacity and dedication it would not be unusual to produce 12 collections a year.

There is no doubt Bernard Arnault respected Galliano's work, and it is easy for an 'ivory tower' syndrome to set in when a designer is so indulged. When billion dollar industries are at stake such designers are mostly, by necessity, divorced from reality. Galliano's Valium habit had become a necessity to balance the stress of the workload, and alcohol was a release. It was under the influence of drugs and booze that Galliano said vile, racist things to people in local bars in the Marais area of Paris where he lived, and a major scandal emerged.

On February 25, 2011 Dior announced that the company had suspended Galliano following his arrest over his alleged anti-Semitic tirade in a Paris bar. The incident happened just before Paris Fashion Week for autumn/winter 2011/2012. Video evidence appeared to show a similar rant in the same bar the previous December. Many friends and colleagues came to his defense, but the damage was done, and Galliano was dismissed from Dior. In September, a Paris court found him guilty of making racist and anti-Semitic remarks, and he

was given a suspended fine.

Fashion's rumour mills have seen any number of designers proposed to take over the reins at Dior, from Raf Simons to Marc Jacobs to Riccardo Tisci, but Galliano's chief pattern cutter of 23 years, Bill Gaytten, seems destined to remain at the helm.

ALEXANDER MCQUEEN

Alexander McQueen gained enormous professional respect over the years, not only for the spectacular shows he presented, but also for the beauty of his work. He seemed to have everything to live for. Voted four times British Designer of the Year, in 2003 he received the CFDA Award for Best International Designer and was honoured with a CBE from Queen Elizabeth II for his services to the fashion industry. But McQueen was left totally bereft and overwhelmed with sadness when his mother died in 2010, following the death of his friend and mentor, Isabella Blow, four years earlier. The dramatic power of Alexander McQueen's fashion vision lives on as the fashion world comes to terms with his tragic death on February 11, 2010 at the age of 40.

In May 2011 the Costume Institute of the Metropolitan Museum of Art in New York staged a retrospective exhibition called *Alexander McQueen: Savage Beauty*, celebrating his work over two decades, and to their astonishment the exhibition produced the busiest opening day in the museum's history. It attracted more than five hundred thousand visitors and had to be extended to accommodate the increasingly large crowds. The exhibition's organiser, Andrew Bolton, an

OPPOSITE Designer Galliano presents a softer look for spring/summer 2007 in the style of the 1930s. A dress in graphic black and white features glossy flower embroidery.

ABOVE A classically beautiful shape and delicate textural embroidery features strongly on this evening dress, by Alexander McQueen, autumn/winter 2005.

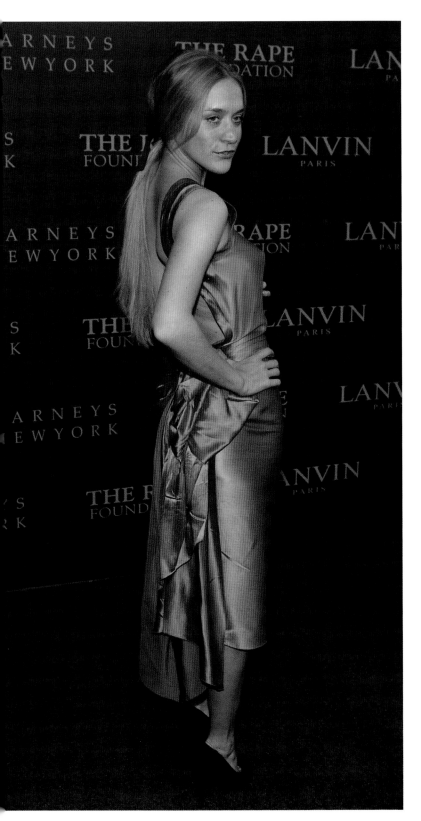

English anthropologist turned museum curator, is convinced that analysing costume offers a powerful key to understanding society. He explained that clothes certainly send out messages about status, identity and so on, but what McQueen was essentially doing with clothes was cutting across cultural boundaries and reordering our ideas. That could explain the raw, mesmerising appeal of his work.

The show arranged examples of McQueen's garments in roughly chronological order, including pieces that McQueen made while still at art school. Boned bodices, Scottish tartans, frock coats, corsets, Napoleonic uniforms, bustles, padded hips, wire crinolines and much more all appear in his collections as quotations from the past, translated by his imagination into something new and fresh and uniquely his own.

THE RESURRECTION OF THE LEGENDARY COUTURE HOUSES

Many of the legendary, but almost forgotten couture houses of Paris reappeared during the first half of the 21st century, some with more success than others. Like a sleeping beauty, the house of Lanvin awoke in 2001 to find her perfect prince in Alber Elbaz. The French have truly embraced this Israeli designer, awarding him the Légion d'honneur and French citizenship in recognition of his rejuvenation of Lanvin.

OPPOSITE Ornithology was Lee McQueen's passion, translated brilliantly in so many of his designs. A model almost takes flight in a red feather design from spring/summer 2000.

LEFT Actress Chloë Sevigny at a benefit in California wearing one of the popular red-carpet satin dresses by Alber Elbaz for Lanvin.

Elbaz became Lanvin's artistic director in 2001 and now no label is more loved and sought after by the best dressed in Hollywood – Gwyneth, Nicole, Sarah Jessica, Charlize – and are all customers for his magically light flyaway dresses. Elbaz relishes the hard work needed to keep all the cogs working smoothly at Lanvin. With his hands-on approach, he manages to accomplish everything and every one of his duties with grace, humour and style. He even attends to the window dressing, adding a touch of his brand of humour here and there.

Nicolas Ghesquière joined Balenciaga when it was owned by Groupe Jacques Bogart in 1995, to design uniforms and wedding gowns for its licensing division. The house had been dormant as a fashion force for nearly 30 years until he was appointed creative director in 1997 at the young age of 25. Known for his fearless and futuristic use of fabrics and silhouettes, Ghesquière's work soon revived Balenciaga as a critically acclaimed ready-to-wear fashion house; and when the Gucci Group took the house over in 2001 they kept him on.

Ghesquière remains in awe of the great Cristóbal saying, "Cristóbal Balenciaga discovered so many things, was so inventive, it's astonishing. I can work on something I think is new and then look back through the archives and find it there already." In 2003 Ghesquière had the idea of launching an *Edition* line based on some of the original iconic pieces. They have been a great success, flying off the racks

as soon as they appear. 'Capsule' collections, derivatives of runway designs, have also been successfully launched and the house now makes a healthy profit. Like the other young designers who have been elevated to creative directors of legendary fashion houses Ghesquière has had to learn that even the most beautiful clothes look better beside a stronger balance sheet.

Ricardo Tisci at Givenchy, Phoebe Philo at Celine, Tomas Maier at Bottega Veneta, Christophe Decarnin at Balmain and Brazilian designer Francisco Costa at Calvin Klein are the newest crop of hot designers who have proven to the delight of their customers and employers that they can live up to their iconic brand names and take them into the highly competitive and fast-moving fashion future with skill and creativity.

Peter Dundas is another glowing example of how to turn a dusty brand around. He is now creative director of Emilio Pucci, the glittery LVMH co-owned Italian luxury label based in Florence and enjoying a 60s and 70s fashion revival.

Norwegian by birth, Dundas was brought up in the US. The former designer at Emanuel Ungaro and right hand to Roberto Cavalli and Jean Paul Gaultier, he has been producing irresistibly sexy collections for the new jet-set. Devoted fans include Eugenie Niarchos and Julia Restoin-Roitfeld. At Valentino, Maria Grazia Chiuri and Pier Paulo Piccioli are making waves with their exquisitely delicate couture collections – all ruffles and femininity but in a modern way.

OPPOSITE Gwyneth Paltrow's red carpet choice for the 63rd Annual Golden Globe Awards was a white embroidered evening dress by Nicolas Ghesquière for Balenciaga.

ABOVE Designer Peter Dundas celebrates with models after a successful showing of his autumn/winter collection for Pucci in Tokyo.

At Chanel, Karl Lagerfeld became the shrinking man, not in professional terms but physically; transformed over 13 months in 2001 from a tubby-looking middle-aged man to a svelte figure dressed as a man half his age. A master of reinvention, he continues to approach his enormous workload of many collections with much vigour. The House of Chanel, jointly owned by Alain and Gerard Wertheimer who are great grandsons of the early (1924) Chanel partner Pierre Wertheimer, is one of the few classic couture houses to remain a privately held business.

THE PASSING OF AN ERA

Valentino Garavani, the flamboyant Italian designer whose client list included practically everyone who was anyone in high society, and who became known for his glamorous red dresses, announced he would retire in January 2008. His partner, Giancarlo Giammetti, had already sold the company for just over $1 billion (£600 million/€800 million) in 1998 to an Italian conglomerate controlled, in part, by the late Gianni Agnelli; and in 2002 it was sold again to Marzotto Apparel, a Milan-based textile giant.

Never one to do things by half, to celebrate his 45th year in fashion Valentino showed his winter 2007 haute couture collection in Rome,

RIGHT The Chanel suit has gone through many changes in the hands of Lagerfeld. For autumn/ winter 2008 decoration was banished, but the hand-woven tweed and braid remained.

OPPOSITE King of glamour Valentino Garavani celebrated 45 years as a designer with a haute couture show in Rome where he first opened in the 1950s.

where it all began for him back in the 1950s. A three-day fashion extravaganza was arranged including balls, dinners and fashion shows. A long list of celebrities and fellow designers attended, including Karl Lagerfeld and Giorgio Armani, Tom Ford and Donatella Versace; the final standing ovation drew tears as well as the signature wave to Frank Sinatra's song *New York, New York*.

Yves Saint Laurent, considered the greatest French couturier of his generation, died in Paris on Sunday June 1, 2008 at the age of 71.

Gucci had bought the YSL trademark back in 1999, but Saint Laurent and Bergé had continued to run the haute couture business. Then, in 2002, Saint Laurent retired from fashion after years of ill health and he and his partner Pierre Bergé closed down the haute couture house. In 2010 a retrospective of his work was held at the Petit Palais in Paris and later at the Denver Art Museum in 2012.

A FASHION FOR CELEBRITIES

Celebrities became our fashion icons in the noughties. A study published by McLachlin & Golding showed that celebrity entertainment stories increased from 6% of the news in the tabloid press in 1952 to 17% in 1997.[2] Magazines completely devoted to what celebrities wear, where they go, what they do and how to get the look are still best sellers.

In fact, by the mid-noughties it was rare to see a fashion model on the cover of the highest profile glossies, unless she was a celebrity in her own right. Actors, singers and even minor celebrities were deemed to be the icons of style. The same applied to advertising campaigns – the higher the profile of the brand, the more famous the actress who was the face of the brand.

A new breed of celebrity was born in 2000 with the first appearance of the reality television series *Big Brother*, which brought together a group of unknowns. Some of its participants became reality stars simply from

OPPOSITE The Ara Pacis Museum in Rome rolled out the red carpet to welcome back Valentino and his signature red dresses.

LEFT Victoria Beckham has found success as a fashion designer. A silk jersey, skin-tight belted dress and weekend bag depict her particular style.

being on the show: we had well and truly entered an age when people who were famous primarily for being famous had crept into the media and the establishment press. On the Internet, sites like As Seen On Screen (asos. com), which started up in 2000, specialised in selling replica and original versions of clothing worn by celebrities, and Cool Spotters (coolspotters.com) provided a one-stop portal to identifying the products, brands and fashions worn by particular celebrities.

Seeing a way to cash in on the act, many celebrities started their own fashion companies; it didn't matter whether they had any training or even if they had little personal style – their name and celebrity status were credit enough. Other celebrities did have the credentials to become successful. After starring in *Sex and the City* with its focus on fashion, Sarah Jessica Parker became a fashion mogul with her own brand and perfume, as well as continuing her acting career. Recently Victoria Beckham's luxury clothing and accessory lines have become much sought after status symbols among the aspirational new rich. She was also awarded a highly prized front page in *Women's Wear Daily* during the spring of 2011. Ex-models Elle Macpherson and Heidi Klum have also established themselves as ace businesswomen and designers.

Former child stars Mary-Kate and Ashley Olsen structured their company, aptly named Dualstar, to catch all levels of the market: The Row at the luxury end, Elizabeth and James as the bigger, contemporary section and Olsenboye as a more accessibly priced range

ABOVE Mary-Kate and Ashley Olsen wear their own designs at the 2011 CFDA Fashion Awards at Alice Tully Hall, New York City.

OPPOSITE From the Roland Mouret autumn/winter 2005 collection in Londo the glamorous 'must have' cocktail dress that became the 'star' of the season.

for teens which reaches the mass market in partnership with J.C. Penney. Originally set up as an investment when the twins were just six years old, the girls took control of the company on their 18th birthday and are now enjoying the rewards of their work building The Row into one of America's highest-ranking luxury goods brands. The line includes flattering feminine trouser suits, corduroy jackets, fabulous coats of every length, and well designed dresses, as well as crazily glamorous furs and the inevitable must-have handbags.

Celebrity consumerism, however, is not exclusive to the 21st century. During the 1930s Hollywood and its stars exerted a huge influence on contemporary fashions and "anything reeking of Jean Harlow is still a top seller," says Christian Madrigal of Thefrock.com

The French designer Roland Mouret's *Galaxy* dress from his 2005 collection must take the prize for most popular celebrity choice and most copied dress of the decade. It was curvy with a low neckline and cap sleeves and made to fit close to the body. Soon A-list Hollywood stars were photographed wearing it – Cameron Diaz, Demi Moore, Rachel Weisz, Scarlett Johansson and Victoria Beckham all embraced the designer and *that* dress.

Mouret explained the inspiration for the dress came from the curvaceous shape of celebrities such as Scarlett Johansson and Dita Von Teese. He explained, "They said 'we have to wear a bra' and all my floaty and drapey stuff, they could not wear so I made a dress for women

RIGHT H.R.H. The Duchess of Cambridge with Prince William after their April 29, 2011 wedding. The wedding dress was a great success in ivory silk and lace designed by Sarah Burton for Alexander McQueen.

who wear bras."[3] As well as producing his own name brands from London, including menswear, Mouret has been named as the next creative director of Robert Clergerie in Paris. The company was bought out from its founder Robert Clergerie by Fung Capital in April 2010 and is undergoing an ambitious expansion.

New celebrity status was acquired by marriage for the Duchess of Cambridge, previously Kate Middleton, who married Prince William in July 2011. Tall and slim with glossy chestnut brown hair and a pretty smile, the Duchess is as glamorous as any supermodel or Oscar-winning actress. Since her marriage in an Alexander McQueen gown by Sarah Burton, the Duchess has been voted one of the best-dressed women of 2011, and is becoming the ultimate ambassador for British fashion, much like the late Princess Diana. The Duchess has stepped out in outfits from British designers Alexander McQueen, Jenny Packham, Alice Temperley, Erdem, Roland Mouret, Burberry and Roksanda Ilincic. Everything she wears starts a trend and sells out fast.

In the 21st century, political wives moved confidently into the spotlight of fashion, glamour and celebrity. Michelle Obama, the first lady of America, has demonstrated a natural and democratic style and is the perfect ambassador for fashion. Her elegant presence and eclectic mixes of high end and High Street is much admired and copied. Former supermodel Carla Bruni's swift rise to first lady of France could not be more pleasing for France's top designers.

LEFT British Prime Minister's wife, Samantha Cameron and first Lady Michelle Obama have a smartly relaxed working style, seen here on a visit to American University in Washington.

And Samantha Cameron, the British Prime Minister's wife, is refreshingly youthful and fashion-conscious.

Lady Gaga used fashion and dressing up as a powerful tool, enabling her to become a megastar. The world's biggest pop star with global sales of 12 million for her 2008 debut album, *The Fame*. In a seemingly endless parade of mostly outrageous costumes, with favourite designers Armani Privé, Alexander McQueen, Prada, Thierry Mugler and Chalayan, she has become the planet's biggest pop phenomenon. *Time* magazine voted her one of the most influential people of 2009. Tiny without her eight-inch heels, the 25-year-old singer, songwriter and performer was born Stefani Joanne Angelina Germanotta in New York City. And fashion loves her.

The first decade of the 21st century saw a stubborn fashion trend that gripped the imagination, if not the ground. Shoes became platforms of art like never before. Heels (and soles) rose to alarming heights, were elaborately decorated and priced outrageously. It was not only on the stage and the catwalks; real women hobbled forth in the name of fashion, six, eight, even nine inches off the ground, launched into the stratosphere on heels of brightly coloured snakeskin or woven raffia. Strapped, backless, or open-toed and wonderful to look at, these shoes empowered the small and made any girl's legs a mile long.

FASHIONABLE MUSEUMS

Museums became the most sought after venues for fashion addicts in the first decade of the millennium. In London the Victoria and Albert Museum kicked off with a Versace retrospective in 2002, followed by *Sixties Fashion* in 2006 and the wonderfully researched 2007 exhibition, *The Golden Age of Couture*. In 2011 it was Yohji Yamamoto's turn with a retrospective designed by Yamamoto's long-term collaborator Masao Nihei that profiled the Japanese designer's career to date, some 30 years after his Paris debut. Record numbers attended for a chance to get up-close to this fascinating designer's work.

At the Musée des Arts Décoratifs in Paris two memorable exhibitions come to mind: the 2009 Madeleine Vionnet retrospective, showing many of her daring and beautifully executed designs up close, and the more recent and fascinating creations of Hussein Chalayan in the *Fashion Narratives* show. The Madame Grès exhibition at the Musée Bourdelle in Paris demonstrated her unique masterful skill with drapery, not only with amazingly fine pleating but also with her modernist asymmetrical shapes, which were always so flattering on the body. Even Buckingham Palace opened its doors to showcase the gloriously romantic Duchess of Cambridge's wedding dress.

The Montreal Museum of Fine Art's Thierry-Maxime Loriot staged a Jean Paul Gaultier retrospective in 2011 entitled *The Fashion World of Jean Paul Gaultier: From the Sidewalk to the Catwalk*, examining how his themes still resonate: multi-culturalism, gender play, the assimilation of the transgressive into designs of real beauty. In 2010 Hamish Bowles curated a relatively small exhibition, *Balenciaga: Spanish Master*, first in New York and then San Francisco, where a series of tableaux explored Cristóbal Balenciaga's breath-taking style in designs that elucidated the master's deeply conservative instincts, strict lines, and affection for uncompromisingly radical mid-century modernist shapes.

ABOVE LEFT Madeleine Vionnet's timeless style - a 1938 neoclassical dress in white muslin and black ribbon and still greatly sought after today.

BELOW LEFT A parade of mannequins demonstrate the fascinating work of Jean Paul Gaultier at an exhibition held at the Museum of Fine Arts in Montreal, entitled *The Fashion World of Jean Paul Gaultier – From Sidewalk to Catwalk.*

RIGHT Floor-length dress and black coat by Yohji Yamamoto decorated with amusing red bobbles, from the autumn/ winter 2004 collection shown in Paris.

VINTAGE FASHION

Looking back has never been so fashion-forward. Pre-worn clothing became part of mainstream fashion and acquired a new name, vintage. Just as in the 1970s, vintage was popular not necessarily because of an economic downturn, but because it was a means of reflecting homogenous mainstream fashion and encouraged individual expression. If you wore vintage you were recognised as a connoisseur and fashion individualist. Magazines devoted precious editorial space to vintage, and celebrities loved it.

The west coast of America became an excellent hunting ground for thrift shops and vintage clothing, benefitting from the closure of many of the costume departments of Hollywood studios. Rita Watnick, the owner of L.A.'s vintage designer clothing shop Lily et Cie, is a well-known supplier of the glamorous Oscar frocks famous for turning starlets into red carpet royalty. By pairing fabulous stars with the right retro-glamorous gown, she has helped transform the way the fashion pack thinks about vintage. She was behind Winona Ryder's memorable white beaded chiffon flapper gown at the 1994 Oscars; Naomi Campbell's Jean Dessès prom-style dress worn at Christie's in London in 1999; and the yellow Jean Dessès dress worn by Renée Zellweger that stole the show at the Oscars in 2001.

RIGHT Jennifer Lopez wears a vintage dress, possibly by French couturier Jean Dessès, bought from the Californian vintage store Lily & Cie for the 78th Annual Academy Awards in 2006.

ABOVE The window
display for the Kate
Moss collection does not
give anything away at
TopShop in Oxford Street.

Kate Moss was a key catalyst; beginning in 2006 she transferred many of her best finds into a Kate Moss range for Topshop, the forward-looking London fashion store. At the higher end, Liberty and Selfridges of London both devoted special areas to vintage couture, as did the Printemps store in Paris.

TheFrock.com in San Francisco specialises in antique, vintage couture and wedding gowns, as well as celebrity wardrobe and memorabilia. "It's all about fabulous frocks that women have worn and loved for their beauty, their details, and flattering silhouettes"[4], owner Christian Madrigal told *Vogue*. In New York, Keni Valenti Retro-Couture is known as 'the King of Vintage'. In Paris, insiders know where to find the best vintage couture and accessories; the jewel-like boutiques owned by Didier Ludot on the Palais Royal house a treasure trove of vintage haute couture. The tiny boutique called

Virginia in London's Notting Hill, is a favourite of Kate Moss and other celebrities.

Actress turned London's vintage queen Virginia Bates has become a bit of a celebrity herself, regularly appearing on the social pages of the glossy magazines and managing to provide a constant supply of vintage clothing of exceptional quality since the 1970s. Saratoga Trunk in Glasgow is Scotland's largest vintage clothing shop with a warehouse that contains original clothing, costume jewellery and props from the Victorian age through every decade to the 1990s.

Vintage fairs have become as much a part of the annual fashion calendar as the biannual prêt-a-porter and textile fairs, and the idea is expanding beyond fashion to homewares, music and dance. Wayne Hemingway of Red or Dead fame stages a large vintage clothing fair in the UK that was first held in July 2010. The event was so successful it was staged the following year in central London's Festival Hall and Embankment, combining vintage bands, clothing, furniture, dancing and crafts stalls, and attracted huge crowds. There are similar events held throughout the US as well as in Scandinavia and other European countries.

There are people who are willing to pay a premium for rare items and historic provenance, collecting costume as an art form; and auction houses have achieved astonishingly high prices for prime costume pieces. In the Christie's sale of 2006, the iconic black couture gown made by Hubert de Givenchy and worn by Audrey Hepburn in the opening scene of *Breakfast at Tiffany's* sold for an astounding

£410,000 ($656,000/€475,000), seven times over the expected price. Even the Edith Head sketches of the same dress fetched £57,600 ($92,160/€66,120) from an estimated value of £11,000–15,000.

Kerry Taylor Auctions specialises in costume and textiles. After a period at Sotheby's, Taylor left to set up her own auction business, specialising in the fields she loves. In her career Taylor has worked on historic, landmark auctions such as the magnificent wardrobes of the Duke and Duchess of Windsor, and the stunning wardrobe of Princess Lilian of Belgium, whose 1950s Diors looked as fresh as the day they were made, complete with matching accessories.

Since the establishment of her own firm she has handled many celebrated collections including those for the Honourable Daphne Guinness, supermodels Jerry Hall and Marie Helvin, and the actress Leslie Caron's collection of haute couture including 1950s Givenchy and 1960s Saint Laurent. Recent sales at Kerry Taylor Auctions saw the knitted mesh slip-dress worn by Kate Middleton at a St. Andrew's University charity fashion show, designed by Charlotte Todd in 2002, sell for £65,000 ($104,000/ €75,000); and an original couture-made Yves Saint Laurent *Mondrian* dress go for £28,000 ($45,000/€32,500).

When the price of vintage garments sky rocketed, it left the stylish shopper faced with a genuine dilemma. Some of the old clothes cost more than the new, which in some cases looked exactly the same; the question was: which is the best investment? Vintage usually means one of a kind, but what makes vintage superior is the construction. The materials were finer and more time generally went into the craftsmanship. Even when a house re-issues a design it is seldom quite right. The colour is off or the silk is different. But with such iconic heritage it would be foolish not to take advantage of in-house archives and reproduce 'classic' pieces. Yves Saint

ABOVE Virginia Bates, vintage clothing boutique owner, popular with models and celebrities, wearing one of her precious 'finds'.

Palace as sources of inspiration.

COLLABORATIONS

At the same time, stores such as Topshop, H&M and Uniqlo became as successful as high fashion brands, encouraging collaborations with designers like Versace, Stella McCartney, Karl Lagerfeld, Celia Birtwell and Jil Sander who added their names and cachet to ranges sold within these stores. Target in the US has had collaborations with designers such as Proenza Schouler, Alice Temperley and Isaac Mizrahi. There was a stampede for Stella McCartney's and Karl Lagerfeld's ranges for H&M in 2005 that were blatantly sold later at a profit on eBay. Kate Moss's debut collection for Topshop had a similar effect, selling out within hours of appearing on the rails.

DENIM ENDURES

Music festivals such as Glastonbury became the chic places to go and to be seen, where festival-goers such as Kate Moss and Sienna Miller were closely observed for fashion trends. Ugg boots became an item, along with patterned Wellington boots, the skinniest blue jeans and the shortest shorts.

The status of denim had no limits. Some blue jeans were so smart they could go to the boardroom such as those designed in silk and denim by Bottega Veneta. Skinny jeans had been shown by fashion designers such as Versace and Stella McCartney in the early 2000s, but the look took hold when it was favoured by Kate Moss and all her wannabes as well as by couturiers such as Karl Lagerfeld. As street-wise as ever, he based the autumn/winter 2011 Chanel ready-to-wear collection around dark

ABOVE Kate Moss has become a style leader for her neat way of putting a look together. Here she fashions her preferred 'rock chic' look.

Laurent, Balenciaga and Dior have all launched collections based on this premise. Ralph Lauren has long sent a team of buyers to Europe in search of authentic country clothes and many designers use specialised vintage outlets such as Saratoga Trunk, Twentieth Century Vintage and denims, pairing them with Chanel-inspired tweedy tunics. Jean Paul Gaultier's inventive take on denim included a beautiful denim evening skirt that was finely shredded at the hem to appear like feathers for the spring 2010 couture collection; but if you were looking for high priced blue jeans it would be hard to top the 1999 Tom Ford *Pocahontas* model for Gucci, embellished with beads, feathers and embroidery, that sold for a cool £2,000 ($3,200/€2,320). It was a kind of rebellious dressing that often went with the beginning of a new century, a sort of fake punk that included a lot of zips, lurex, leather and lace.

FINANCIAL GROWTH
IN THE LUXURY BUSINESS

"If the world economy could survive on handbags alone, we would have emerged from the latest recession a while ago"[5], said the London *Times* in June 2011. Handbags became one of the biggest (in size as well as sales) status symbols of the decade. Victoria Beckham designed a one-off bag for Selfridges costing £8,995 ($14,390/€10,435). The lucky girl who receives one of these über-luxurious bags can always auction it for double the price and buy herself a small car!

Every luxury brand has its best seller, but none more than Mulberry. When Mulberry recruited a former Burberry handbag designer, Emma Hill, as its creative director in 2008, the *Bayswater* bag represented 40% of the company's sales. When Hill spotted Alexa Chung carrying around an old Mulberry *Elkington* men's briefcase, she immediately set about designing a new bag in her honour.

The *Alexa £785* sparked an 18,000-person waiting list and now rivals the *Bayswater* for sales – and so it goes on. With handbags selling for more than £500 ($800/€580) (and much more if you want one made in skin

OPPOSITE Slender fashionista Alexa Chung has quite a following, and frequently appears in glossy magazines. Photographed holding one of her favourite Mulberry bags.

RIGHT It is not just clothes that are sold on the catwalk today but a brand's whole range including accessories. Christopher Kane, designer at Burberry Prorsum, produces the 'total' look in abundance.

usually found in zoos), the 40-year-old company quadrupled its profits in 2011 to £23.3 million ($3.73 million/€27 million), raising its status to a super brand.

Another traditional British brand to experience enormous financial success is Burberry. Christopher Bailey is the shrewd and stylish Yorkshireman at the design helm of the firm, and has succeeded in transforming the traditional British clothes manufacturer into one of the most sought after international brands. Bailey joined Burberry in 2001 and made radical changes, bringing the business into the 21st century and rejuvenating the products to appeal to a younger, more affluent market. Burberry saw a 21% growth in the last financial year , exceeding £1 billion ($1.6 billion/€1.1 billion) for the first time.

In a conversation with Colin McDowell in the *Times*, Bailey admitted unpretentiously, "Burberry is much bigger than I am, it's 153 years old. My life here hasn't even reached ten years yet, but I have been here long enough to say that Burberry flows in my veins. I love its values. I respond to its strong foundations and, of course, its history is a constant inspiration."[7]

THE NEXT GENERATION OF DESIGNERS

In the ever-changing world of fashion the new generation of designers – and there are many, from all corners of the globe – are off

RIGHT Belgian designer Haider Ackermann's pared down style in brilliant jewel coloured silks provides a modern attitude to fashionable dressing.

OPPOSITE Cumbrian-born designer Giles Deacon's clothes stand out from the crowd, such as this elegant floor-length red satin evening dress from his spring/summer 2012 collection.

to a promising start. Among those who have already found an impressive level of success: Christopher Kane for Versus, Haider Ackermann, Dries Van Noten, Erdem, Philip Lim, Narciso Rodriguez, Jonathan Saunders, Michael Kors and Giles Deacon, Thakoon Panichgul and Jason Wu to name but a few.

At first the Dutch duo Viktor & Rolf were considered to be fashion outsiders when they appeared on the scene in 1993. Viktor Horsting and Rolf Snoeren funnelled their ideas of clothing as art through the medium of fashion, expressing abstract ideas and concepts. An early example of this expression of clothing as art was their fashion presentation entitled *Babushka* (autumn/winter 1999-2000), where a lone model, Maggie Rizer, was positioned on a revolving platform to be dressed by the designers in nine garments, one on top of the other like a Russian doll in reverse. Their quirky style has gained popularity over the years and with a desire to expand they entered into a partnership with Italian clothing magnate Renzo Rosso of Only the Brave in 2008, allowing the company to develop new product ranges and open further boutiques. Viktor & Rolf bring our attention to the changing and broadening scope of fashion, and though their designs may not always be commercial, they certainly suggest that clothing can be

considered in a different way.

Sarah Burton succeeded Alexander McQueen upon his death in 2010. She had joined the company in 1996 as an intern, and subsequently returned after her graduation from Central St. Martins in 2000 to become head of womenswear, acting as McQueen's aide until his final days in the studio. As design director, the collection she produced directly after his death was a fitting tribute and gained worldwide praise. The collection included brocade jackets, elegant organza and lace dresses and sumptuous chinoiserie-inspired gowns in black and gold that caught the eye of Kate Middleton, now Duchess of Cambridge, who chose Burton to design her wedding dress when she married H.R.H.Prince William in July 2011.

It is encouraging that with enough talent and tenacity it's still possible to succeed in the US fashion industry without the financial backing of a multi-million dollar conglomerate. With a sophisticated and demanding audience, fashion designers Jack McCollough and Lazaro Hernandez, who graduated from Parsons in 2002, realised early success by reading their target market accurately and producing collections with a grounded sportswear sensibility.

California-based sisters Kate and Laura

OPPOSITE An evening shift dress from Rodarte's autumn 2000 collection in white silk overlaid with sheer, shimmering silver sequins.

ABOVE A whimsical evening tuxedo by the Belgian designers Viktor & Rolf, from the spring/summer 2007 ready-to-wear.

Mulleavy, founders of the label Rodarte, are relative newcomers to the list of respected fashion designers. Since arriving in New York in the spring of 2005 to show their collection to buyers and influential fashion editors, they have gone from strength to strength receiving prestigious awards and gaining a loyal following. Known for their meticulous attention to detail, their garments combine an element of deconstruction as well as old style couture. Their romantic dresses bring an artisanal feel to fashion. US *Vogue* approved, commenting "that finally, an American collection had redefined red-carpet dressing – a whole new take on American elegance," adding that the sisters are increasingly creating clothes that will work not just from an editorial perspective but for a pragmatic wardrobe as well. In addition, they designed some of the costumes for the movie *Black Swan* (2010).

INTO THE FUTURE

The new millennium also saw the beginnings of a movement towards responsible consumption, using fabrics and materials with less impact upon the environment. Vintage and secondhand clothing, along with handcrafted and repurposed or up-cycled pieces, were prized by those with more individual, eclectic tastes; they were just as often mixed with celebrity, high-fashion pieces as well as with high-street fashions and denim. In a new millennium, it would seem, anyone could be a designer or stylist.

ABOVE Full-length, leaf print chiffon dress with textured silver leather belt, by Sarah Burton for Alexander McQueen from the spring/summer 2011 collection.

OPPOSITE Few designers understand red carpet dressing more than the Rodarte sisters. Guaranteed to be noticed, any star would be happy to wear one of their beautifully crafted gowns.

8 Clicking Away

In the 21st century, digital technology has changed the way we shop, research information and explore trends, giving the consumer a newfound power. Now anyone could publish, connect with like-minded others, share, collaborate and develop an audience or a market.

The Internet shopping company, Net-a-Porter, started by the former journalist Natalie Massenet in June 2000, has been highly successful. Massenet started the company following a fruitless search for a pair of perfectly fitting designer jeans. Net-a-Porter is aimed at the affluent and fashion-conscious consumer she knew was out there. Her dream was that even if you lived in the most remote outpost of the world, you could still have the latest fashion delivered to the door. The website shows the latest trends and has its own on-line magazine as well as offering the latest clothing, accessories, shoes and bags to customers across the globe.

In 2010 Massenet sold her remaining stake in the company to Swiss luxury goods group Richemont and pocketed a cool £50 million ($80 million/€58 million).[1] Since then the company has mushroomed, and currently has an estimated turnover of around £120 million ($190 million/€140 million) and 600 employees in London and New York. Massenet taught the fashion world that on-line shopping works, spawning an industry that spans categories and price points. It is a way a lot of women want to live and shop now. On-line fashion auctions such as Gilt Groupe offers time-limited discounts on luxury items, while eBay is a source for finding the occasional bargain. As fashion moves so fast, what seems like a bargain before lunch can be a charity shop dud by tea-time.

OPPOSITE A giant Chanel poster in Shanghai, the richest city in China, where luxury stores have mushroomed in the past few years.

RIGHT Natalie Massenet lives up to her image as fashion entrepreneur of the decade, photographed at the Net-a-Porter headquarters.

THE ECONOMIC ENVIRONMENT

China went from being the sixth largest economy to the third largest with increasingly well traveled, well educated and well off consumers. But according to a report by Bain & Company tastes are changing away from the obviously recognisable luxury brands. In 2010 Louis Vuitton, Chanel and Gucci were the three most desired fashion labels in China. But Hermès is also up there in the top ten and two of the top five womenswear brands are Armani and Max Mara, both the epitome of understated style.[2]

At the time of going to press, Barack Obama was preparing to run for a second term as President of the United States. And while the US economy was showing signs of recovery from the global financial recession triggered by the sub-prime mortgage collapse in 2007, the UK and other countries have yet to make even a partial recovery. Other countries, including the United Arab Emirates, Australia, Brazil and

ABOVE The Gucci store opened in Wuhan, China in July 2009. Followed by Cartier, Hermès, Fendi, Loewe, Ferragamo and Max Mara.

Russia, benefited from the increased demand for their mineral and energy resources that global growth generated. However, the "War on Terrorism" and the war in Afghanistan continue and the so-called Arab Spring is still spreading throughout the Middle East. World peace may not be achieved, yet more people have a voice through social networking sites such as Twitter and Facebook.

With the huge jump in broadband and free Internet portals like YouTube (launched in 2007), Hulu, and Internet TV software solutions such as Joost, a new marketing opportunity has appeared which enables firms to accurately target their market. Many young entrepreneurs have produced alternative TV video broadcasts, some with millions of followers and a growing number of serious advertisers. Called 'vloggers', they can get millions of views a day. In fact, YouTube reports that more than four billion videos are viewed every day on its site.

THE BLOGGERS

It is a sign of the times when fashion designers are so impressed by 'bloggers' they are given coveted front-row seats at their fashion shows. Such was the case with Tavi Gevinson, the American fashion blogger who began her blog *Style Rookie* in 2008 at the age of 11. With a passion for fashion, her parents did not know what Tavi was doing until she asked their permission to appear in a *New York Times* magazine story.[3] Articulate and honest, she was one of the first personal style bloggers to have been truly embraced by the industry. She became a regular guest at Paris shows and a muse for designers in Tokyo.

Gevinson once described herself as a "tiny 13-year-old dork that sits inside all day wearing awkward jackets and pretty hats," but many obviously looked to her for style inspiration. However, it seems that lately she has been looking to other places for a creative outlet and for inspiration. The fashion obsessive has

obviously realised her limitations, but whatever she decides to do in the future she has made an indelible mark on the fashion world and that can't be a bad thing on a girl's CV.

Bryanboy is the pen name of Bryan Grey Yambao, a Filipino fashion blogger. Typical of the generation who grew up on computers and living on virtual time, he started blogging at age 17 from his parents' Manila home. His blog attracts thousands of hits a day. In 2007 he won the Philippine Blog Award for Best Fashion & Lifestyle Blog, and has been named as one of the hottest Internet celebrities by *The New York Post*. His blog, called "hysterically camp" by the *Sydney Morning Herald*, is known for its witty and often bitchy commentary.[4] Marc Jacobs even went so far as to name a handbag after him (the *BB* ostrich bag), and Uniglo advertise with him.

There are so many of these operators, it's hard to keep up; but there are plenty of retailers looking. Notcouture, for example, carries news stories on emerging and cool designers. There are also numerous trendspotting sites such as

FAR LEFT Bryanboy arrives in resplendent style at the Dolce & Gabbana spring/summer 2012 fashion show in Milan.

LEFT The ever-watchful blogger of 'The Satorialist' Scott Schuman, photographed at a book-signing event in Spain.

Streetpeeper, Facehunter and The Sartorialist who focus on street fashion and include photographs of everyday people whose style they admire. Scott Schuman who created The Sartorialist website has also had a book of his photographs published and exhibitions of his work. These sites can be inspirational for designers and put them in touch with what people are wearing on the street – without having to leave the studio.

A consumer can be a designer, buyer or retailer on dozens of sites. An enthusiastic young designer can even finance a collection on Kickstarter. Anyone can be a fashion critic on websites such as Polyvore.com by enabling them to put magazine-style fashion spreads together. The sets can be compiled from items of clothing from all over the Web. Then you share the looks with friends and they can tell you whether they love it or hate it. The more followers you have the more addictive it becomes. There is Farfetch.com, an Internet mall of forty boutiques; Collete.fr, the site of a hip Parisian fashion store; and Brownsfashion. com the London luxury mini-chain, and many more. It is a bit like playing paper dolls with pictures of real clothes.[5]

DIGITAL TECHNOLOGY

Digital technology has revolutionised fabric design; practically any print effect, proportion or texture is achievable. Designers are seeking inspiration from previously unexplored sources,

LEFT London-based designers Basso & Brooke demonstrate how a patchwork of classic prints on satin can light up the catwalk, from autumn/winter 2012.

and a new visual language for surface design is starting to evolve. The cross-disciplinary use of graphics programmes, digital photography, video and special effects is no longer the preserve of the young avant-garde but is seen more and more in mainstream fashion. Issey Miyake, Hussein Chalayan and Comme des Garçons are just a few of the designers who have been instrumental in leading the way.

Not only are the new techniques more economical than traditional screen, hand printing or embroidery methods but there are seemingly no limits to what can be achieved in terms of design and texture – trompe l'oeil, three dimensional surfaces and overlay effects can be engineered onto any form. Advances in UV and latex inks are able to produce clear, bright colour divisions. New advances in machinery have made synthetics such as polyesters look and feel as good as couture quality duchesse satin, and stretch silks have given designers more freedom to manipulate and explore different silhouettes.

Three seasons into the second decade of the 21st century and it's a time when textile and print designers are having their fashion moment. A panoply of fascinating prints dominate at all price points. Outstanding talents have emerged from Central Saint Martins in London, such as

RIGHT A summer dress with peplum bodice in landscape print of fauna and leaves, by design duo Christopher de Vos and Peter Pilotto, familiarly known as Peter Pilotto.

Lauren McCalmont who graduated with an MA and has produced dazzling prints for Peter Pilotto, Louise Gray and Calvin Klein and whose sporty digital prints will soon be appearing on Asos.com's eveningwear line. All kinds of prints have appeared – the brighter and bolder, the better. At Balenciaga medieval stained glass windows were Nicolas Ghesquière's inspiration whilst pale pastel blossoms were spread all over Roberto Cavalli's suits and dresses, but the most column inches went to Mary Katrantzou, London's hottest print superstar, and her sharp three piece trouser suits smothered with multi-coloured fields of flowers.

Mary Katrantzou trained in America for a BA in architecture before transferring to Central Saint Martins to complete a BA degree in textile design. Since graduating in 2008, her riotous prints in intense colours and strong couture shapes have thrust her firmly onto the international fashion stage. Her thematic collections revolve around an icon of luxury, an object from art or design that a woman would not be able to wear if it were for real: perfume bottles, Fabergé eggs, 18th century paintings and interiors. In November 2011 Mary was awarded the British Fashion Award for Emerging Talent and in February 2012 Young Designer of the Year at the Elle Style Awards.

LEFT Adventurous and uplifting floral prints layered to form a neat tailored look were a great success for Mary Katrantzou in the autumn/winter season of 2011.

She had already designed a capsule collection of handbags and totes for the luxury French firm Longchamp and has been working with the renowned Parisian embroidery house of Lesage, a first of its kind collaboration with a London designer. Sadly, the founder, Francois Lesage, passed away in 2011.

ETHICAL FASHION

Along with new technologies and their possibilities, there are other global issues that have come to the forefront in the 21st century. One such issue is the impact of the industry on the environment. The fashion industry has been criticised for its emphasis on new trends and cheap, throwaway fashion by people concerned about the impact of industry practices on both the physical and social environment. In the past, with a few exceptions, the words ethical and fashionable didn't go together and the clothing was considered worthy but not fashion-forward. That is no longer true.

Ethical fashion, as defined by the Ethical Fashion Forum (www. ethicalfashionforum. com); "represents an approach to the design, sourcing and manufacture of clothing which maximizes benefits to people and communities while minimizing impact on the environment."[6] This has become increasingly important to the industry and more attention is being paid

OPPOSITE Lauren McCamont's Africana prints are striking on Scottish designer Louise Gray's dress, from the runway show for the autumn/winter 2012 collection in London.

LEFT A brilliant yellow ruffle hem dress from the autumn/winter 2012 collection of Mary Katrantzou.

to where clothing is manufactured, to using processes that minimise or eliminate pollution, to reducing water usage and recycling materials where feasible. For example Nike, who had been strongly criticised both for water pollution and for using sweatshops to produce their wares, is committed to ensuring their workers are treated fairly and to adopting a waterless systems for textile dying.

There are, of course, many designers for whom ethical fashion and sustainable design is nothing new. Concern for animal welfare and other ethical issues have always informed Stella McCartney's designs. She is known for not using leather or fur in any of her collections. Katharine Hamnett has also always been very direct in her views on ethical and environmental issues. She is also leading the way for developing organic supply chains.

Vivienne Westwood has created a collection of handbags using recycled material as part of a collaboration with The Ethical Fashion Programme working with marginalised women in Nairobi, Kenya.

Scientists are also developing new ways of creating materials. For example, it has long

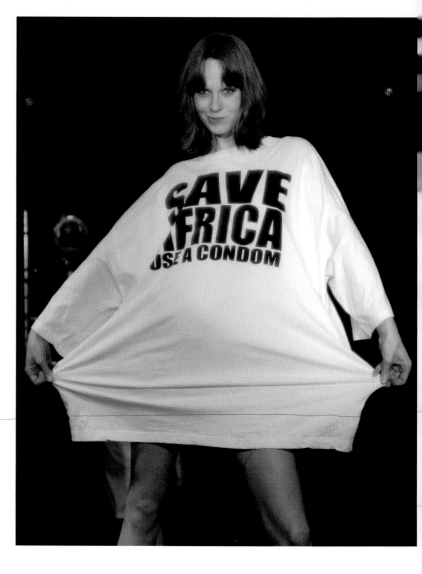

RIGHT Katharine Hamnett is a great believer in wearing her heart on a T-shirt. This one is a protest against the spread of AIDS in Africa.

ABOVE RIGHT Vivienne Westwood proudly displays her eco-friendly shopping bags.

OPPOSITE Bianca Gavrilas models one of two capes made from the golden silk of 1.2 million orb spiders. They took two men in Madagascar eight years to make. Photographed at the Victoria & Albert Museum.

been known the spider's silk is incredibly strong, but is difficult to use in any quantities due to the spiders' propensity for killing each other. The golden cloth spun by orb spiders displayed at the American Museum of Natural History in New York City and also at the Victoria & Albert Museum in London involved one million spiders, many workers to harvest the silk and took four years to create. It is a beautiful piece, but clearly not a viable way to produce cloth on a larger scale. On the other hand, silkworms are much easier to farm and are more prolific. Dr. Donald Jarvis, of the University of Wyoming in the US, and his colleagues introduced an element of spider silk into silkworms that have then incorporated it into their own silk production. The benefits of being able to create stronger silk goes far beyond fashion and has applications in medicine and as a greener substitute for toughened plastics which require a lot of energy to produce according to an article by Pallab Gosh on the BBC website.

THE GLOBAL FASHION INDUSTRY IN THE 21ST CENTURY

The fashion industry is huge globally. In the US alone it has been estimated at close to $200 billion ($125 million/€160 million). According to Morss Global Finance, the estimated expenditure worldwide for clothing is in the region of $1.22 trillion ($770 billion/€975 billion).[7]

RIGHT A shimmering silver silk evening dress based on the lines of the all-time American classic –dungarees– by Ralph Lauren for the spring/summer 2010 New York collection.

OPPOSITE Dolce & Gabbana's typically lavish use of lace embroidery. Corset dress in black and gold Sicilian-style pattern from the autumn/winter 2012 collection shown in Milan.

British fashion has always dared to be different with a reputation for being a breeding ground for innovative design. But now more than ever its designers are serious contenders in the world market, producing slick, beautifully made and wearable clothes and raising an annual £21 billion ($33.5 billion/€24 billion) in revenue for the country.

Fashion designers around the world have created fabulous works In endless variations for their collections during the past few years. Prints have made - and continue to make - a big impact. Experiments with metallic fabrics shimmered and shined for a couple of seasons giving clothes a glamorous new twist and now it is lace, (in all its forms) turn to cast its magic – chunky guipure at Dolce & Gabbana and Marc Jacobs, embroidered lace at Valentino, stenciled on shoes and jewellery at Yves Saint Laurent, lacquered at Tom Ford and laser printed at Clements Ribeiro and Erdem.

WHAT GOES AROUND... COMES AROUND

As the Justin Timberlake song suggests "What Goes Around…Comes Around" and as this book comes to an end we are clinging as never before to the familiar in matters of style.

Fashion is working the 40s frock, the 70s midi skirt lengths, 60s shifts and tunics in abundance. In the shops and on the street you can see vintage coat shapes, dramatic floral prints and couture styling reminiscent of the 1950s. The TV series *Mad Men* became the cult show of the decade – not so much for the characters or the story, more for the wardrobe – and sent fashion designers once more into fifties and sixties mode. Jewel and noon colours, androgynous dressing and lady-like pencil skirts, along with the glamorous metallic and shiny textures of the 1920s and 1930s persist. They all continue to parade catwalks around the world – it seems the future has arrived but fashion is all about dreaming of the past with a twist.

For many of today's fashion enthusiasts these designs will look entirely new, and they will experience the pleasure of wearing them in just the same way as their mothers, grandmothers and possibly great-grandmothers did.

Whether coming from the street, from vintage collections, celebrity-inspired, pasted together by young bloggers, or created in the rarified atmosphere of high fashion, new inspiration will emerge to create the next phase of fashion history.

OPPOSITE A romantic and timeless 1950s evening dress with infanta bodice of scroll embroidery and pale pink tulle skirt, by Cristóbal Balenciaga.

Chronology of Designers

Among the European design houses, designers often moved from one house to another. The connections especially among the established French houses are fascinating. Interestingly, there is not the same level of movement between different companies in the US or in the UK. Although in the last decade or so, there have been a number of key appointments of UK-trained designers to the French fashion houses. Here is a small selection of some of these connections (in alphabetical order):

FOUNDED BEFORE 1950	SOME OF THE MAJOR DESIGNERS WHO WORK THERE
Cristóbal Balenciaga (1895–1972) Founded 1937	André Courrèges, Valentino Garavani, Nicolas Ghesquière, Hubert de Givenchy, Emanuel Ungaro
Pierre Balmain (1914–1982) Founded 1945	John Cavanagh, Christophe Decarnin, Karl Lagerfeld, Oscar de la Renta
Céline (Céline Vipiana) Founded 1945	Michael Kors, Phoebe Philo
Coco Chanel (1883–1971) Founded 1909	Karl Lagerfeld, Julien Macdonald
Jean Dessès (1904–1970) Founded 1937	Valentino Garavani, Guy Laroche
Christian Dior (1905–1957) Founded 1946	Azzedine Alaïa, Marc Bohan, Pierre Cardin, Gianfranco Ferré, John Galliano, Herbert Kasper, Yves Saint Laurent, Raf Simons
Jacques Fath (1912-1954) Founded 1937	Valentino Garavani, Hubert de Givenchy, Herbert Kasper, Guy Laroche
Guccio Gucci (1898–1953) Founded 1921	Tom Ford, Frida Giannini
Norman Hartnell (1901–1979) Founded 1923	Marc Bohan, Gina Fratini, Victor Stiebel, Yuki
Jeanne Lanvin (1867–1946) Founded 1909	Alber Elbaz, Claude Montana
Edward Molyneux (1891–1974) Founded 1919	Pierre Balmain, Geoffrey Beene, Marc Bohan, John Cavanagh
Jean Patou (1887–1936) Founded 1919	Marc Bohan, Jean Paul Gaultier, Christian Lacroix, Karl Lagerfeld
Emilio Pucci (1914–1992) Founded 1948	Peter Dundas, Christian Lacroix, Matthew Williamson

FOUNDED IN THE 1950s AND 1960s

Geoffrey Beene (1927–2004)
Founded 1963

Alber Elbaz, Issey Miyake, Kay Unger

Pierre Cardin (1922–1993)
Founded 1950

Jean Paul Gaultier

Chloé (Jacques Lenoir & Gaby Aghion)
Founded 1952

Karl Lagerfeld, Stella McCartney, Hannah MacGibbon, Phoebe Philo, Martine Sitbon

André Courrèges (1923–)
Founded 1961

Jean Charles de Castelbajac, Emanuel Ungaro

Hubert de Givenchy (1927–)
Founded 1952

Ozwald Boateng, John Galliano, Julien Macdonald, Alexander McQueen, Issey Miyake, Riccardo Tisco

Anne Klein (1921–1974)
Founded 1968

Donna Karan, Richard Tyler

Guy Laroche (1923–1989)
Founded 1956

Azzedine Alaïa, John Cavanagh, Alber Elbaz, Michel Klein, Valentino Garavani, Issey Miyake

Yves Saint Laurent (1936–2008)
Founded 1962

Alber Elbaz, Tom Ford, Stefano Pilati

Emanuel Ungaro (1933–)
Founded 1966

Jean Charles de Castelbajac, Peter Dundas

FOUNDED IN THE 1970s AND 1980s

Perry Ellis (1940–1986)
Founded 1978

Tom Ford, Marc Jacobs

Jean Paul Gaultier (1970–)
Founded 1976

Peter Dundas, Nicolas Ghesquière

Christian Lacroix (1951–)
Founded 1987

Peter Dundas, Stella McCartney (intern)

Footnotes

INTRODUCTION

1. & 2. Ernestine Carter, **Magic Names of Fashion**, (London: Weidenfeld & Nicolson, 1980) P. 93
3. Christian Dior, **Dior by Dior: The Autobiography of Christian Dior**, (London: V & A Publications, 2007) p. 26
4. Jane Mulvagh, **Vogue History of 20th Century Fashion** (New York: Viking Press, 1988) p 181
5. "High Fashion: The Paris Designers", **Time Magazine**, 4 March 1957, p. 33

CHAPTER 1

1. & 2. Christian Dior, **Dior by Dior: The Autobiography of Christian Dior**, (London: V&A Publications, 2007), p. 22
3. & 4. Diana Vreeland, **D.V.**, (New York: Alfred A. Knopf, 1984), p. 106
5. Judith Thurman, "The Absolutist", **The New Yorker**, 3 July 2006, p. 60
6. Lesley Miller, senior curator of textiles, Victoria & Albert Museum.
7. Diana Vreeland, *ibid.*
8. Marie Andree Jouve and Jacqueline Demornex, **Balenciaga**, (London: Thames & Hudson, 1989), p. 19
9. Pamela Golbin, **Balenciaga Paris**, (London: Thames & Hudson, 2006), p. 31
10. Gloria Emerson, "Balenciaga The Couturier, Dead at 77", **New York Times**, 23 March 1972
11. "Balenciaga the Great", **The Observer**, 13 October 1985, p. 51
12. Hardy Amies, **Still Here: an Autobiography**, (London: Weidenfeld & Nicolson, 1984), p. 85

CHAPTER 2

1. Edna Woolman Chase, editor of **Vogue**, on Vionnet
2. & 3. Christian Dior, **Dior by Dior**, trans. Antonia Fraser, (London: V&A Publications, 2007), p. 62
4. Lesley Ellis Miller, **Balenciaga**, (London: V&A Publications, 2007)
5. Gloria Emerson, "Balenciaga The Couturier, Dead at 77", **The New York Times**, 23 March 1972

6. Sarah Tomerlin Lee, **American Fashion: The Life and Lines of Adrian, Mainbocher, McCardell, Norell, and Trigere**, (New York: Quadrangle/New York Times Book Co, 1975), p. 211
7. & 8. **Time** magazine, 10 August 1953
9. Frances Kennett, **Secrets of the Couturiers**, (New York: Orbis Books, 1986), p. 57
10. & 11. Prudence Glynn, The Times, 3 August 1971

CHAPTER 3

1. *Bonnie Cashin Foundation*, www.bonniecashinfoundation.org
2. *Mary Quant: A New Approach, Chelsea 1955-67, sixties fashion display*, Victoria & Albert Museum, www.vam.ac.uk
3. Barry Miles, **The British Invasion: The music, the times, the era**, (New York: Sterling Publishing, 2009)
4. Ernestine Carter, on Mary Quant, **The Sunday Times**
5.–8. *Interview with Foale & Tuffin* , Victoria & Albert Museum, www.vam.ac.uk
9. Avis Berman, Jack Cowart and Michael Lobel, **Roy Lichtenstein: All About Art**, (Louisiana Museum of Modern Art, 1999) p. 8
10. Barbara Hulanicki, **From A to Biba: An Autobiography**, (London: V&A Publications, 2007)
11. Lydia Kamitsis, **Paco Rabanne**, (London: Thames & Hudson, 1999)
12. Shirley Kennedy, Pucci: **A Renaissance in Fashion**, (New York: Abbeville Press, 1991), p. 86
13. & 14. "Marc Bohan: Agent Provocateur", **Women's Wear Daily**, 1967

CHAPTER 4

1. Alice Rawsthorn, **Yves St Laurent: A Biography**, (New York: HarperCollins Publishers, 1997), p.111
2. Carol Troy and Catherine Milinaire, **Cheap Chic**, reprinted from an interview with YSL originally from *Oui Magazine*. (New York: Harmony Books, 1975), pp. 57-58
3. Caroline Baker, **Nova**, April 1970, p. 77
4. Ernestine Carter, **Magic Names of Fashion**, (London: Weidenfeld & Nicolson, 1980)
5. Ossie Clark lecture at the Royal College of Art, 1996
6. **Vogue**, October 1976, p. 210

CHAPTER 5

1. Bridget Foley, **WWD: 100 Years, 100 Designers** (New York: Fairchild Publications, 2010)
2. Nina Hyde, **The Washington Post**, quoted in *Armani Press book*, October 1987
3. *Donna Karan Press Release*, winter 1988
4. Hamish Bowles, **Yves Saint Laurent: Style**, (New York: Harry N. Abrams, 2008) p. 472
5. Hamish Bowles, *ibid*, page 9

CHAPTER 6

1. "People", **Newsweek**, 4 March 1996, p. 60
2. The National Centre on Addiction and Substance Abuse at Columbia University, *Women under the Influence* (Baltimore: Johns Hopkins University Press, 2006) p. 98
3. Jacob Sullum, "Victims of Everything", **The New York Times**, 23 May 1997
4. Mark Holgate, "Interview with Helmut Lang", **Vogue (US)**, September 2010, p. 392
5. Sarah Mower, "Helmut Lang U.S.A.", **Harper's Bazaar**, September 1998, p. 526
6. Mark Holgate, *ibid*, p. 404

CHAPTER 7

1. Suzy Menkes, "The Collections/Paris: Dior is big, bright and bold", **The New York Times**, 4 March 2004 (www.nytimes.com/2004/03/04/news/04iht-rdior ed3 .html)
2. Shelley McLachlan and Peter Golding, "Tabloidization in the British Press: A Qualitative Investigation into Changes in British Newspapers, 1952-1997", in C. Sparks and J. Tulloch, **Tabloid Tales: Global Debates Over Media Standards** (New York: Rowman & Littlefield, 2000)
3. Polly Vernon, "Sexy's Back", **The Observer**, 2 August 2009 (www.guardian.co.uk/lifeandstyle/2009/aug/02/fashion-designers-fashion)
4. Sally Singer, "The Frock.com" (interview with Christian Madrigal), **Vogue**, December 2005
5. Luke Leitch, "Berry that turned itself into cream of the crop", **The Times**, 17 June 2011, p. 15

6. Colin McDowell's interview with Christopher Bailey at **The Sunday Times Style In Conversation** series, 24 September 2009

CHAPTER 8

1. Alexandra Topping, "Natalie Massenet sells Net-a-Porter stake to Richemont for £50m", **The Guardian**, (www.guardian.co.uk/business/2010/apr/01/net-porter-massenet-richemont)
2. **The Times: Luxx Magazine**, 10 March 2012, p. 50
3. Maysa Rawi, "Move over Geldof girls: Meet Tavi, 13, the blogger with the fashion industry at her feet", **The Daily Mail on-line** www.dailymail.co.uk/femail/1215048
4. Andrew Hornery, "PS Catwalk", **Sydney Morning Herald**, 3 May 2008
5. Alexandra Jacobs, "Fashion Democracy: The world of virtual Anna Wintours", **The New Yorker**, 29 March 2010
6. Ethical Fashion Forum (www.ethicalfashionforum.com)
7. "The Global Economics of Fashion and Clothing: Part 2—Fashion", Morss Global Finance (www.morssglobalfinance.com)

Bibliography

BOOKS & CATALOGUES

Baudot, F., **A Century of Fashion**, (London: Thames & Hudson, 1999)

Bluttal, S. and P. Mears, **Halston**, (London: Phaidon, 2011)

Bowles, H., **Balenciaga and Spain: Spanish Master**, (New York: Rizzoli International, 2011)

Breward, C., **Fashion (Oxford History of Art)**, (Oxford: Oxford University Press, 2003)

Breward, C., D. Gilbert and J. Lister, **Swinging Sixties**, (London: V&A Publications, 2006)

Brubach, H., **A Dedicated Follower of Fashion**, (London: Phaidon, 1999)

Buxbaum, G., **Icons of Fashion**, (London: Prestel, 2005)

Carter, E., **20th Century Fashion: A Scrapbook – 1900 to Today**, (London: Eyre Methuen, 1975)

Cawthorne, N., **The New Look: The Dior Revolution**, (London: Hamlyn, 1996)

Chang, J., **Can't Stop Won't Stop. A History of the Hip-Hop Generation**, (London: Ebury Press, 2007)

Connike, Y., **Fashions of a Decade: The 1960s**, (Falmouth: Chelsea House Publishers, 2007)

Cosgrave. B., **Costume & Fashion: A Complete History**, (London: Hamlyn, 2000)

Foley, B., **WWD: 100 Years, 100 Designers**, (New York: Fairchild Publications, 2010)

Glynn, P. and M. Ginsburg, **In Fashion: Dress in the Twentieth Century**, (London: Allen & Unwin, 1978)

Gorman, P., **The Look. Adventures in Rock & Pop Fashion**, (London: Adelita, 2006)

Herald, J., **Fashions of a Decade: The 1970s**, (Falmouth: Chelsea House, 2006)

Hillman, D. and D. Gibbs, **NOVA: 1965–1975**, (London: Pavilion Books, 1993)

Jaeger, A-C., **Fashion Makers Fashion Shapers: The Essential Guide to Fashion by Those in the Know**, (London: Thames & Hudson, 2009)

Keenan, B., **Dior in Vogue**, (London: Octopus Books, 1981)

Lagerfeld, K., **Karl Lagerfeld: Fotograf—Photographer—Photographe**, (Cologne: Benedikt Taschen, 1990)

Laurent, Y.S., **Yves Saint Laurent**, (London: Thames & Hudson, 1984)

Laver, J., **Costume and Fashion: A Concise History**, (London: Thames & Hudson, 1969)

Mackenzie, M., **Isms: Understanding Fashion**, (London: A & C Black Publishers Ltd, 2009)

de Marly, D., **Christian Dior**, (London: Batsford, 1990)

McDowell. C., **Galliano**, (New York: Rizzoli International, 1998)

Mendes, V., **Pierre Cardin: Past, Present, Future**, (3Nishen Publishing, 1990)

Milbank, C. R., **New York Fashion: The Evolution of American Style**, (New York: Harry N. Abrams, 1989)

Milbank, C. R., **Couture: The Great Fashion Designers**, (London: Thames and Hudson, 1985)

Okonkwo, U., **Luxury Fashion Branding: Trends, Tactics, Techniques**, (London: Palgrave Macmillan, 2007)

Palomo-Lovinski, N., **The World's Most Influential Fashion Designers**, (London: A & C Black, 2010)

Polhemus, T., **Street Style**, (London: Thames & Hudson, 1994)

Salazar, L., **Yohji Yamamoto**, (London: V&A Publishing, 2011)

Snow, C. W., **The World of Carmel Snow**, (New York: McGraw-Hill Book Company Inc, 1962)

Tilberis, E., **Vogue 75 Years**, (New York: Conde Nast, 1991)

Turner, A. W., **Biba: The Biba Experience**, (Woodbridge: Antique Collectors' Club, 2007)

Vercelloni, I. T., **Missonologia: Il Mondo Dei Missoni**, (Milan: Mondadori Electa, 1994)

Versace, G. and O. Calabrese, **Versace Signatures**, (New York: Abbeville Press, 1992)

Watson, L., **20th Century Fashion: 100 Years of Style by Decade and Designer, in Association with Vogue**, (Ontario: Firefly Books, 2004)

Watt, J., **Ossie Clark 1965–1974**, (London: V&A Publications, 2003)

Wilcox, C., **The Golden Age of Couture**, (London: V&A Publications, 2008)

Yohannan, K. and N. Nolf, **Claire McCardell: Redefining Modernism**, (New York: Harry N. Abrams, 1999)

MAGAZINES & NEWSPAPERS

Condé Nast is an international organisation whose publications include *Vogue* magazine, published in various editions in over 24 countries. Other fashion-related magazines that they publish include *Glamour*, *GQ* and *W*, all of which are aimed at the consumer. They also own Fairchild Fashion Media, the leading source of information about the fashion industry for fashion professionals. This group includes *WWD (Women's Wear Daily)*, *Style.com*, *FN (Footwear News)*, among others.

Harper's Bazaar is owned by Hearst Publications and was America's first fashion magazine. During its almost 150 years of existence, it has been home to a number of legendary fashion editors: Carmel Snow, Diana Vreeland and Alexey Brodovitch are some of the best known. Diana Vreeland left *Harper's Bazaar* to work for *Vogue*. Editions of *Harper's Bazaar* are published in 27 countries.

There are many other on-line and print sources of information on fashion and the fashion industry available in addition to the ones mentioned above. *Drapers* is a UK-based journal and website (www.drapersonline.com) for the industry. In France, there is *Journal du Textile* and the Union Francaise des Industries de l'Habillement, which is the trade association for the clothing industry, as well as the famous Chambre Syndicale de la Haute Couture. In Germany there are *Textil Wirtschaft* and *Textil Mittellungen*. Similar publications and organisations exist in most countries active in the fashion world.

WEBSITES & BLOGS

The following websites and blogs are just a small sample of the on-line resources available:

Museums and auction houses:

The Metropolitan Museum of Art, New York: www.metmuseum.org
The Victoria & Albert Museum, London: www.vam.ac.uk
The Design Museum, London: www. designmuseum.org
Musée des Arts Décoratifs –Musée de la Mode et du Textile, Paris: www.lesartsdecoratifs.ft
Galleria del Costume, Florence: www.uffizi.firenze.it
Balenciaga Fashion Museum, Getaria, Spain: www.cristobalbalenciagamuseoa.com
Museum at the Fashion Institute of Technology, New York: www.fitnyc.edu
The Kyoto Costume Institute, Japan: www.kci.or.jp
Kerry Taylor Auctions, London: www.kerrytaylorauctions.com
Christie's: www.christies.com
Sotheby's: www.sothebys.com

General fashion:

The fashion model directory has brief biographies of many fashion designers: www.fashionmodeldirectory.com
The British Fashion Council: www.Britishfashioncouncil.co.uk
London Fashion Week:www.londonfashionweek
www.vogue.com
www.weconnectfashion.com
www.fashionista.com
www.fashiondirectory.com
www.milanfashionweek.com
www.cameramoda.it
www.parisfashionweek.com
www.modeaparis.com
www.newyorkfashionweek.com
www.wmagazine
www.wired.com

Blogs

Twonerdyhistorygirls.blogspot.com
Tavi Gevinson: www.Thestylerookie.com
Bryanboy: www.bryanboy.com
Scott Schuman: www.thesartorialist.com
Permanent Style (men's fashion): www.permanentstyle.co.uk
Tokyo Fashion (Japan): www.tokyofashion.com
Anna Dello Russo (Italy/Japan): www.ammadellorusso.com
Les Mads (Germany): www.lesmads.de

Index

Picture Credits

While every effort has been made to credit the appropriate source, if there are any errors or omissions please contact us and we will make corrections in the next printing.

From a private collection, drawing by Nino Caprioglio, pp 7, 123; © Keystone-France/Gamma-Keystone via Getty Images, pp 8, 9, 30; © John Chillingworth/ Getty Images, p 10; Courtesy of Mr. Ian Thomas L.V.O., p 12; © Pat English/ Time-Life Pictures/Getty Images, p 11, 13, 20; © Erwin Blumenfeld/Condé Nast Archives/ Corbis, p 14; © Mary Evans/Hearst Magazines UK, pp 15, 16, 18, 19, 25, 31, 32, 33, 38, 39, 40, 42, 47, 56, 60, 67, 70, 74, 89, 90, 91, 92, 94, 96, 99, 102, 108, 109, 110, 112, 248, 277; © Genevieve Naylor/Corbis p 17, 61, 63; © Victoria and Albert Museum, pp 21, 24, 26, 29, 34, 36, 43, 45, 57, 71, 100, 103, 114, 128, 135, 136, 137, 163, 174; © Bettmann/ Corbis, p 22, 62, 80, 154, 177; © Gjon Mili/Time-Life Pictures/Getty Images, p 27; © Walter Sanders/Time-Life Pictures/Getty Images, p 28, 44; © Horst Horst/Condé Nast Archive/Corbis, p 35; © Apic/Getty Images, p 37; © John French/V&A Images, pp 41, 65, 95, 97, 98; © Kammerman/Gamma-Rapho via Getty Images, p 48; © dpa INP/ dpa/Corbis, p50; © Keystone/Getty Images, p 51, 69, 87; © Gordon Parks/Time-Life Pictures, p 53; © Clifford Coffin/ Condé Nast Archives/Corbis, p 55; © RDA/Getty Images, p 58, 126; © Epic/ Mary Evans Picture Library, p 59; © Studio Patellani/Corbis, p 66; © Loomis Dean/Time-Life Pictures, p 68; © Frank Horvat/Condé Nast/Corbis, p 73; © Lipnitzki/Roger Viollet/Getty Images, p 75; © Gene Lester/Getty Images, p 76; © George DeSota/Newsmakers/Getty Images, p 77; © Eliot Elisofon/ Time-Life Pictures/Getty Images, p 78; © Frances McLaughlin-Gill/Condé Nast Archive/Corbis, p 79; © Rose Hartman/Getty Images, p 81, 199; © Henry Clarke/Condé Nast Archives/Corbis, p 82; © Nina Leen/Time-Life Pictures/ Getty Images, p 83; © John Cohen/Getty Images, p 84; © Fred Mott/Getty Images, p 85; © GAB Archive/Redferns, p 86, 139; © Bob Thomas/Getty Images, p 88; © Popperfoto/Getty Images, p 101; © Justin de Villeneuve, p 105, 119; © Keystone Features/Hulton Archive/Getty Images p 107; © Mary Evans Picture Library/James Eadie, p 106; © Reg Lancaster/Getty Images, p 111; © Courtesy Edwin Co Ltd. The registered trademarks Fiorucci®, Fioruccino®, Fiorucci Safety Jeans®, Fiorucci Time® and the 'angels' (figurative trademark) are owned by Edwin Co Ltd. There are neither ownership nor license connections between these trademarks and Mr. Elio Fiorucci, p 115; © Paramount/Getty Images, p 117; © Blank Archives/Getty Images, p 118; © Hulton Archive/Getty Images, p 120; © Dave M. Benett/Getty Images, pp 121, 252; © Gail Mooney/Corbis, p 122; © Arnaud de Rosnay/Condé Nast Archive/Corbis, p 124; © Catwalking, pp 125, 164, 186, 187, 197, 200, 205, 208, 212, 221, 226, 238, 243, 256, 257, 258, 268, 272b; ©Francesco Scavullo/Condé Nast Archive/Corbis, pp 127, 148; © Peter Still/Redferns, p 129; © Michael Putland/Getty Images, p 130; © Justin de Villeneuve/Hulton Archive/Getty Images, p 131; © Courtesy of the Laura Ashley Estate, p 132; © Ian Gavan/Getty Images, p 133; © Courtesy of Fashion Museum, Bath, p 134; © Erica Echenberg/Redferns, p 138; © Ted Thai/Time-Life Pictures/ Getty Images, p 140; © Tim Jenkins/Condé Nast Archive/Corbis, p 143; © Courtesy of the Valentino PR Office; © Michael Ochs Archives/Getty Images, p 145; © 1977, United Artists, Courtesy of Tony Nourmand, p 146; © Ron Galella/WireImage, pp 147, 156, 191; © Studio Systems Ltd, exclusively for Browns, 1981, pp 149, 150; Advertisement for Calvin Klein®, 1980, p 151;

© Louie Psihoyos/Corbis, p 153; © Catherine Karnow/Corbis, p 155; © Thomas Iannaccone/Condé Nast Archive/Corbis, p 157; © News (UK) Ltd/Rex Features, p 158; © Sygma/Corbis, p 159; © Julian Calder/Corbis, p 160; © Al Freni/Time-Life Pictures/Getty Images, p 162; © Olycom SPA/ Rex Features, p 165; © Nick Gutteridge/View Pictures/Rex Features, p 166; © Pierre Vauthey/Sigma/Corbis, pp 167, 172, 175, 178, 185, 194; © Rex Features, p 168; © Dave Benett/Getty Images, p 170, 214t; © Daniel Simon/ Gamma-Rapho via Getty Images, p 171, 219; © Peter Turnley/Corbis, p 179; © Stephen Wright/ Redferns, p 180; © Julio Donoso/Sygma/Corbis, p 182; © Pierre Guillaud/AFP/Getty Images, p 184; © Frank Micelotta/Getty Images, p 188; © Dave Hogan/Getty Images, p 189; © Jim Smeal/WireImage, p 192; © News (UK) Ltd/Rex Features, p 193; ©Time Graham/Getty Images, p 195; © Vittoriano Rastelli/Corbis, p 196; © Franco Origlia/Getty Images, p 198; © Pierre Verdy/AFP/Getty Images, p 201, 225, 227, 233, 259; © Michel Arnaud/Corbis, p 202; © Kyle Ericksen/Condé Nast Archive/Corbis, p 204; © John Aquino/Condé Nast Archive/Corbis, p 206; © Emmanuelle Sardella/Condé Nast Archive/Corbis, p 207; © Wood/Rex Features, p 210; © Steve Wood/Rex Features, p 211; © Sinead Lynch/AFP/Getty Images, p 213; © Imaginechina/Corbis, p 214b; © Most Wanted/Rex Features, pp 215, 217; © Frederic Reglain/Gamma-Rapho via Getty Images, p 216; © Dave Corio/Michael Ochs Archive/Getty Images, p 218; © Thomas Coex/ AFP/Getty Images, p 220; © Ken Towner/Evening Standard/ Rex Features, p 222; © Marcel Thomas/FilmMagic, p 228; © Jean-Pierre Muller/AFP/Getty Images, p 230; © Jean-Pierre Muller/AFP/Getty Images, p 231; © Antoine Antonio/Bloomberg via Getty Images, p 232; © Cavan Pawson/Evening Standard/Rex Features, p 234; © Vince Bucci/Getty Images, p 235; © Kevin Winter/Getty Images, p 236; © Jun Sato/WireImage, p 237; © Eric Vandeville/ Gamma-Rapho via Getty Images, pp 239, 240b; © Victor Virgile/Gamma-Rapho via Getty Images, pp 241, 267, 271; © Kevin Mazur/WireImage, p 242; © Carl de Souza/AFP/Getty Images, p 244; © Andrew Parsons/Hmages, p 245; © Francois Guillot/AFP/Getty Images, pp 246, 249, 260; © Canadian Press/Rex Features, p 248b; © Frazer Harrison/Getty Images, p 250; © Harold Cunningham/ WireImage, p 251; © Neil Mockford/FilmMagic, p 253; © Ray Tamarra/Getty Images, p 254; © Damien Meyer/AFP/Getty Images, p 255; © JP Yim/WireImage, p 261; © Liu Jin/AFP/Getty Images, p 262; © Richard Young/Rex Features, p 263; © China Photos/Getty Images, p 264; © Jemal Countess/Getty Images for Y-3, p 265; © Jacopo Raule/Getty Images, p 266lft; ©Juan Naharro Gimenez/Getty Images, p 266rgt; © Paul Cunningham/Corbis, p 269; © WWD/Condé Nast/Corbis, p 271; © Vivienne Westwood, Ethical Fashion Africa, p 272; © Adrian Dennis/AFP/ Getty Images, p 273; © Emmanuel Dunand/AFP/Getty Images, p 274; © Venturelli/WireImage, p 275

ACKNOWLEDGEMENTS

Special thanks to my mother and to my family. Also to Lee Ripley, publishing director at Vivays for working so tirelessly with me on this project. Thanks also to Gem Hoahling and David Paton, David Cutts and Vinny Lee. Apologies to those whose names are not included — they are nevertheless sincerely thanked for their help and we are and shall remain extremely grateful to them. I also want to thank Ian Hunt for his patience.